PUDUMAIPPITTAN

OUR RECENT RELEASES

Short Fiction

Ayoni and Other Stories
Edited and Translated by Alladi Uma
& M Sridhar

Home and Away
By Ramachandra Sharma Translated by Padma and Ramachandra Sharma

Katha Prize Stories 10
Ed. Geeta Dharmarajan
& Nandita Aggarwal

Forsaking Paradise: Stories from Ladakh,
Edited and Translated by
Ravina Aggarwal

Hauntings: Bangia Ghost Stories
Edited and Translated by Suchitra
Samanta

Vyasa and Vighneshwara
By Anand
Translated by Saji Mathew

Joginder Paul: Sleepwalkers Translated
by Sunil Trivedi and Sukrita Paul
Kumar

ALT (Approaches to Literatures in Translation)

Ismat: Her Life, Her Times
Eds. Sukrita Paul Kumar & Sadique

Translating Partition: Stories, Essays,
Criticism
Eds. Ravikant & Tarun K Saint

Vijay Tendulkar

Trailblazers

Paul Zacharia: Two Novellas Translated
by Gita Krishnankutty

Ashokamitran: Water
Translated by Lakshmi Holmström

Bhupen Khakhar: Selected Works
Translated by Ganesh Devy, Naushil
Mehta & Bina Srinivasan

Indira Goswami: Pages Stained with
Blood,
Translated by Pradip Acharya

Katha Classics

Basheer Ed. Vanajam Ravindran Masti
Ed. Ramachandra Sharma Mauni Ed.
Lakshmi Holmstrom Raj-a Rao Ed.
Makarand Paranjape

Katha Novels

Singarevva and the Palace
By Chandrasekhar Kambar Translated
by Laxmi Chandrashekar

Padmavati
By A Madhaviah
Translated by Meenakshi Tyagarajan

YuvaKatha

Lukose;s Church
Night of the Third Crescent
Bhiku's Diary
The Verdict
The Dragonfly
The Bell

BalKatha

The Carpenter's Apperentice
The Nose Doctor
Grinny the Green Dinosaur
Battling Boats

FORTHCOMING

Daar se Bichchudi
By Krishna Sobti
Translated by Smita Bharti

Ai Ladki
By Krishna Sobti
Translated by Shivnath

Surajmukhi Andhere Ke
By Krishna Sobti
Translated by Pamela Manasi

PUDUMAIPPITTAN

TRANSLATED AND EDITED MY LAKSHMI HOLMSTROM

KATHA

First published by Katha in 2002

Copyright © Katha, 2002

Copyright © for the English translations
rests with KATHA.

KATHA
A3, Sarvodaya Enclave
Sri Aurobindo Marg, New Delhi 110 017
Phone: (91-11) 4141 6600, 4141 6610
Fax: (91-11) 2651 4373
E-mail: marketing@katha.org
Website: http://www.katha.org

KATHA is a registered nonprofit organization
devoted to enhancing the joy of reading.
KATHA VILASAM is its story research and resource centre.

Cover Design: Geeta Dharmarajan
Cover Painting: K S Kulkarni
Courtesy: Gallerie Ganesha
Inside Illustrations: Maradu Trotsky
Inside Photographs and Illustrations Courtesy: Kalachchuvadu

General Series Editor: Geeta Dharmarajan
In-house Editors: Gita Rajan, Shoma Choudhury

Typeset in 12 on 16pt ElegaGarmnd BT by Sandeep Kumar at Katha

Katha regularly plants trees to replace the wood used in the making of its books.

ISBN 978-81-87649-53-3

First Reprint 2009, Second Reprint 2016

Pudumaipittan (Cho Vrittasalam)
25 April, 1990 – 30 June, 1948

Pudumaippittan's parents:
V. Chokkalingam Pillai and Parvathammall.

Pudumaippittan and his wife Kamala.

Pudumaippittan

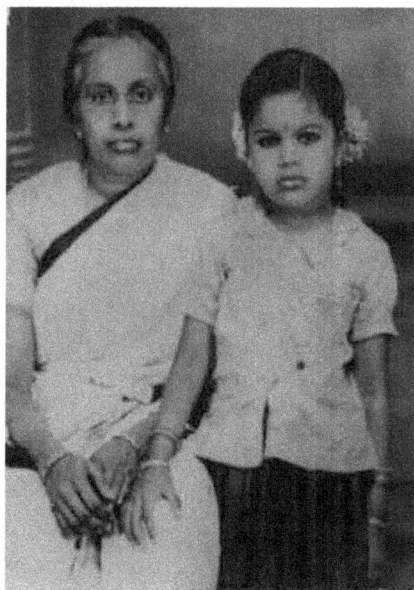

Pudumaippittan's daughter, Dinakari.

CONTENTS

Chronology Bibliography Map

acknowledgements

many people have been of crucial help in the making of this book. In particular, I would like to thank Sundara Ramaswamy, novelist and critic, for sparing the time to discuss Pudumaippittan's stories with me in detail. It was a privilege to share his valuable and stimulating insights. My thanks to M S for reading the drafts of these translations so carefully, and for his comments, and to Paula Richman for her comments on "Deliverance from the Curse" and the story of Ahalya.

The critical essay at the end of the book ("Making it new") was first given as a paper at the School of Oriental Studies, University of London. I am grateful to Stuart Blackburn for inviting me to do this, and for his comments. A later version was published in *South Asia Research*, volume 20, number 2 (Autumn 2000).

Original source texts for this edition were drawn from a documentation project on Pudumaippittan done by the Kalachchuvadu Trust, Nagercoil, with a grant from the India Foundation for the Arts (IFA), Bangalore, with funds underwritten by the Sir Ratan Tata Trust. A R Venkatachalapathy and R Sundaram very kindly allowed me to consult the most reliable texts. I am also indebted to them for the photographs in this book, and for their input to the bibliography and biographical notes.

And I thank my husband, Mark, for his unfailing support.

introduction

why is pudumaippittan relevant to readers today? In the first place, he is rooted in the Tamil country and its culture, and has an important place in Tamil literary history. He was very aware of being part of the Tamil renaissance which began with Subramanya Bharati and others at the turn of the nineteenth century, and of the new perspectives he and his colleagues on the literary journal *Manikkodi* were bringing to the Tamil short story in the 1930s and 1940s. In the second place, he began writing at an important moment in India both in terms of literary and political history. He was born in 1906 and began his literary career in 1934, when Premchand was at the end of his life. Thus the fourteen years during which he wrote happened to coincide with the new Progressive Writers' Movement. Premchand himself, Ismat Chugtai, Mulk Raj Anand and Thagazhi Sivasankaran Pillai were among his great contemporaries. Although Pudumaippittan was not directly part of the Progressive Movement, he shared with these writers their social concerns and their attempts to present these in realistic fiction. But Pudumaippittan was also aware of being part of a yet wider Modernist Movement which included French, Russian, American and English writers as well as Indian, with whom he shared a passion for questioning and restating traditions that had thus far been accepted easily, both in literature and in life.

Pudumaippittan was a writer who engaged fully with contemporary life and times. In this he differed from (and complemented) his great contemporary, Mauni. Mauni's stories are about the life of the mind and its imagination. Pudumaippittan's stories reflect vividly the history of his times, the urbanization of Chennai, social change and mobility, the migration of his own community both to Chennai and to Sri Lanka and their alienation there, the spread of new political ideologies, the influence in Tamil Nadu of Subramanya Bharati, Gandhiji and Periyar. All these are seen with a finely observant as well as a sharply critical eye.

But primarily the stories reflect Pudumaippittan's own felt experience. He wrote, in the introduction entitled "Warning!" to his collected stories *Kanchanai*, in 1943,

> These stories were not written as the result of a vow to bring about cultural uplift, nor as a kind of service to the reading public. They are merely stories. Neither I nor my stories have the least desire to save the world or

to enrich our culture. This is an anthology of episodes reflecting what I have heard, seen, dreamt, wanted to see, and also what I have not wished to see.

Hence the stories come out of his own life, and out of his insights about the community he knew best, the Saiva vellalas or pillais of Tirunelveli District – their tragedies, their dreams and their fantasies. Rooted as they are in the Tamil Nadu of their times, they also touch the timeless and the universal. It is this dual quality that the novelist Sundara Ramaswamy is referring to when he writes that "Chellammal" is one of the greatest of love stories in modern Tamil writing.

During his short working life, Pudumaippittan wrote nearly a hundred stories as well as numerous articles, reviews, poems and plays. Much of this material has now been made available to us through the inspired work of A R Venkatachalapathy and the editors of Kalachchuvadu Press. All readers of Pudumaippittan should be grateful to them and to the two publications, *Annai Itta Thi* (Uncollected and Unpublished Writings of Pudumaippittan), Kalachchuvadu Pathippagam 1998, and *Pudumaippittan Kathaigal* (The Complete Stories of Pudumaippittan: A chronological, variorum edition with critical notes and appendices), Kalachchuvadu Pathippagam 2001.

In this collection of Pudumaippittan's work in English translation I have brought together some of his best known stories, which give some indication of his broad range of content and form. These include some of the short, stark poetic pieces dating from his earliest work, "Street Lamp"; a story with supernatural overtones, "Kaanchanai"; a modern re-working of an ancient tale, "Deliverance from the Curse"; a narrative of proto magic-realism, "God and Kandasami Pillai"; and several deeply reflective stories of contemporary life in Chennai, "Chellammal" et cetera. Every reader of Pudumaippittan will have her own favourite stories. These are mine. The article "About Tamil" was included because it gives us an insight into his balanced position regarding the future of Tamil, and his own preference for the living, richly colloquial language which he uses so well in his own stories. Pudumaippittan's reviews are always succinct and at the same time insightful. Those included here show his grasp of central issues to do with language and translation which anticipate, in quite a remarkable way, the debates in our own times.

A critical essay and overview of Pudumaippittan comes at the end of this book. But first, the stories.

August, 2002   Lakshmi Holmström

Pudumaippittan's stories were originally published in Tamil in various magazines and journals.

At Katha, there has been a conscious attempt to avoid using Indian words as local colour but to use them frequently and unobtrusively as they actually *are* used by most of us. Thus we have deliberately chosen not to italicize Indian words since we believe these belong and should belong to the English language as spoken and used in different parts of India. A few words have been glossed and the meaning or relevant information provided in a footnote in the belief that this information would bring alive the context of the story. Some words have been explicated, in the text, the first time the word is used.

street lamp

at the end of the street, just where it turns a corner, a municipal street lamp stands.

It stands alone, all by its solitary self, trying to spread its dim light.

But youth, old age and death are not the prerogatives of human beings alone. And so, this street lamp had reached its old age.

Its once upright stone body leaned a little. The glass shade upon its crown was broken on one side. When the small boy threw his stone in play, did he think of the lamp's afflictions?

When the wind blows now, does it carry away the lamp's life in a single sweep? No, it kills slowly, leaving the lamp with a fluttering, quivering half life.

"Theruvilakku" was first published in *Oozhiyan* in 1934.

Why can't the wind be grateful that the lamp sheds a little light at least?

Now the wind has gone. And who cares whether the lamp feels the cold or the rain?

Is the wind aware of this?

Now they say there is no need for the lamp in these parts. So they must take it away.

It has a friend. An old man.

Isn't it most likely that those who are equal in age will be friends? What is surprising in this?

For the lamp, an old man.

For the old man, a lamp.

They are going to remove the lamp. The old man doesn't know it though.

Yet how is he to know?

Doesn't he have to beg to fill his belly?

Can he live on an empty stomach?

The street lamp was truly his friend.

Its light gave him such peace of mind.

He came there one evening.

There was only an empty hole there.

Darkness! Darkness!

He was like a blind man whose staff has been knocked out of his hand.

His world became a void that day, a wasteland without meaning.

Peace?

Where would it come from?

It was only a broken street lamp. Yet

it had always consoled him a little.

Even when there was no light, he could at least feel the comfort of its touch under his fingers.

Next day they saw an old man's corpse lying there.

Now there is a new lamp.

An electric lamp.

Beneath it children play eagerly.

What do they care about the old man and the old lamp?

One day they too will go the same way. So what?

Always, everywhere, it is the same.

What is old must end; what is new must begin.

That is the nature of the world.

Pudumaippittan

the human machine

sri minakshisundaram pillai was a
clerk in a grocery store. By the use of grocery scales and account
sheets, he had, in his time, learnt to gauge the tragedies of the
human race and the strange processes of the human mind.

For the past forty five years, his destiny had been the same –
the same path, the same house, the same daily irritations at
the grocery store. What is more, in former days, it used to be
just Ramu's shop at the street corner. But the shop had grown
with Pillaiyavargal. The interesting thing here is that although
the once simple "Minatchi" had been transformed into Sri
Minakshisundaram Pillai, he still ate his frugal meals and
wore the same lacklustre veshtis with their single line border.
The lime and plaster facade and thatched roof of the shop had

"Manida Yandiram" was first published in *Manikkodi* in 1934.

disappeared, giving place to such status symbols as reinforced concrete, electric lights and a shop counter. The shop and Pillai grew together. But they did not grow alike. The shop's income and expenses grew, so did Pillaiyavargal's worries.

Sri Minakshisundaram had a way of resolving miraculously all the problems arising out of the shop's credit and debit accounts. In the old days, he would sit up as late as twelve at night, wrestling by the pedestal oil lamp. His struggle is no less these days – but now the electric fan and light keep vigil with him. His salary too has run with the speed of a tortoise, and reached the heights of twenty rupees a month. But Sri Minakshisundaram Pillai's skills as an expert accountant have stayed within the bounds of the grocery store. As for his domestic accounts, they have gone far beyond even his magical skills. In the past forty five years they have grown in length, like Perumal's stride as he measured the world, they are growing even now.

Every morning at five o'clock, you may see his feet, still covered in sand, turning in great haste from the riverside into Rajappaattai, and from there, once again into the street known as Ottrai Theru.

These past forty five years he has been seen, in rain and in mist, walking along in this way, his wet veshti held aloft in his hands, floating backwards to dry in the wind, his partially wet forehead ablaze with vibhuti from the Subramanya Swami temple, sandal paste and kumkumam. People were not that bothered about the extent of his devotion. He reminded them only of a well wound and faultless machine that had been set in motion.

As soon as it struck six, he walked towards the shop, wearing the veshti and upper cloth that had been washed and dried the day before, combing out the tangles of his still wet hair. You would see him again, at ten or twelve at night, locking up and setting off for home.

Even before Minatchi attained the status of store accountant it had become a common sight to see four or five baby Minatchis engaged in a deep study of different varieties of street dust.

Pillaiyavargal was a patient man. It is said that Adiseshan only carries the weight of this single world. But Pillai carried the burden of a huge planetary system made up of responsibility, betrayal, self-respect and trust, which seemed to swirl about without any established rules. His only gains from his burdensome employment were a receding forehead, a balding crown, a hunched back, and a potbelly acquired from sitting hours on end at his accounts desk.

Pillaiyavargal was a mild man. He had put up with the kicks and blows of ostentation, pride, wealth and arrogance for so long that at last he had entirely lost the will to act, the strength to oppose, and even his own self-confidence. He had resolved that since he was a humble person, he should be circumspect, and always protect himself by holding on to the virtues of truth and trustworthiness. Yet, in that heart of his, which he kept as carefully controlled as a cobra in its box, desire had spread monstrously, like Alladdin's genie, until it had enveloped and occupied his entire heart and will. No devotee will worship the demon desire with full sacrificial rites as fervently as the man who can no longer protect himself.

Appa, this mind that we possess! Yes, Sri Minakshisundaram too possessed such a mind. Vedantists compare important subjects to the ash strewn embers of a fire. Going according to this image, Sri Minakshi would certainly qualify as a great man. Many people tended to say of him, dismissively, "Minatchi? Such a naive man." They would even say it to his face. Yet in such a naive creature's heart, desire smouldered and smoked. He wanted to buy a cow and calf so that his children should not lack for milk, and at the same time – why not – he could sell some of it and earn a few paisa. He wanted to return the Madeover land to Maavanna of South Street. And that wasn't all. He wanted his own store, and another Minatchi, so that he could sit at ease with his legs crossed, and order him about in exactly the same way that others ordered him about now. He wanted to make at least one visit to Colombo, and return with all ceremony, complete with gold waist chain, a fob watch, a handsome figure, plenty of cash in hand, and the title, Colombo Pillai. He wanted everyone who came towards him in the street, to tie their upper cloths around their waist, and ask humbly, showing their teeth all the while, "Annacchi, are you well?" He wanted every marriage that was celebrated, and every funeral that occurred, to seek his presence before proceeding on its course.

So many more wishes! The daily handling of money was entirely his responsibility. And he was always the last to lock up the shop and leave. At that very moment, in the railway station which was within calling distance from the shop, the Tuticorin Shuttle train would set off after its five minute stop. He could easily buy himself a ticket and make a getaway in the dead of night. As far as the fare was concerned, there was always enough money for that from the shop's daily takings. But then there was that police fellow. At the very thought of him, fear struck at Pillai, as if the policeman's hand had come down on his shoulder. Startled, he would actually turn round to see.

Some people wear a watch on their wrists in order to tell the time. Others tend to make use of the way shadows fall. But it is possible for the mainspring of a watch to break down. And if the sun is hidden, the signs made by the shadows will be lost in midair. Perhaps it was because of all this that for most people of Kokkirakulam, Sri Minakshisundaram Pillai was like a well wound clock, a sun that is never hidden by clouds, an unfailing and eternal object.

Pillai was measured in all things. All his activities were like laws of nature, today was exactly the same as yesterday, and so it would be tomorrow and thereafter. And I will say one thing more. Even to the oldest inhabitant of Kokkirakulam he never appeared in anything other than his country veshtis with their fine black line edging. He never swerved from this propriety, nor would he wish to do so.

And even though Sri Pillaiyavargal's face did not reflect any problematic Tejas et cetera, he was a philosopher in his own way. The daily accounts revealed life's secrets to him, and taught him a darkened philosophy, like a light through a smoky lamp.

Even the lampposts on Mulai Theru were exhausted. This was a customary illness which struck the lampposts of Kokkirakulam by ten o'clock at night.

Every other shop along Mulai Theru had closed down. A single electric light shone above the desk in the store. Pillaiyavargal sat on a palm leaf mat making entries into a note book. Subbu Pillai, is it? Four, four and a half, four and a half maagaani, four and a half maagaani and one challi, four and a half maagaani one challi and one duttu, five, nine, five challi! What do we gain by giving credit to the useless wretch! Let him come tomorrow, I'll tell him good and proper. What about Kovalayyan? You can neither talk to him, nor do anything with him. What's to be done? Pillai will have to take care of him.

He riffled through the pages. Wiping off the sweat streaming from his forehead, he turned to the page entitled Ramayya Pillai and began to add, Visam, one eighth, half and one eighth ...

Maavadiya Pillai came in, saying, "What, Annacchi, haven't you shut up shop yet? What are you examining so minutely?"

"Come in and sit down," said Pillai, returning to his accounts.

"What, ayya, the train must have left by now. And you're still at it. Are you crazy?"

"Thambi, you still owe us for three and a half visam, don't you? It's been several days. Please see to it. How can we manage the shop, unless the money comes in?"

"So what, ayya, I'll see to it this coming Thursday. Just give me a visam measure of punnaikkai oil now. I'll pay for everything together."

"Make sure you do it." As he said this, he threw his upper cloth over his shoulder and stood up. He wanted to yawn. Snapping his fingers in front of his mouth, and muttering, "Mahadeva, Mahadeva," he walked up to the copper vessel, green with the verdigris of ages, in which the punnaikkai oil was kept. Before stooping down, he shook his hair out, gathered it all up with his left hand and tucked it away and then filled the visam measure and returned, holding it between thumb and middle finger.

"Thambi," he said, holding out the oil.

Maavadiya Pillai received it in his small brass tumbler.

Pillai folded up his upper cloth and placed it next to his desk. Then, calling out "Mahadeva" and leaning one hand against the desk, he lowered himself gently, to sit on the ground cross-legged.

It didn't seem as if Maavadiya Pillai was in a hurry to leave.

"Well, Annacchi, isn't it time to go yet?" he asked, helping himself to the roasted gram that stood on a platter by the desk and munching.

"I have to look at one or two more entries before I shut up shop. Time will go fast enough. Of course, you are doing all right, it seems. Radhapuram Pillai is starting a money lending business next Vaikasi?"

"What does he lack? He could start a money lending business if he wants to, or he could have a company shop. Anyone can do as they please, if they have the means. Next Vaikasi, is it? Who told you?" He tossed a salted gram into his mouth as he said this.

"What ayya, how can you spread your hands as if you don't know a thing about it? Can anything happen in the Pillai household without your knowledge? So when are you going to let the cat out of the bag?" Minakshisundaram Pillai picked up his pencil, and finding it blunt, began to peel away the wood with his nails.

But Maavadiya Pillai was not prepared to Open his bag that easily. "Why should we listen to the town gossip? I'll be off. It's getting late." And he picked up his oil and prepared to leave.

"Thambi! Don't forget about Thursday," said Minakshisundaram Pillai.

"As if I would," returned Maavadiya Pillai as he disappeared into the darkness.

After this Minakshisundaram Pillai could not concentrate on the accounts. His imagination began to expand on the money lending business that Radhapuram Pillai was about to set up, and of the position there that Maavadiya Pillai was likely to acquire.

What does Maavadiya Pillai lack? Money is always passing through his hands. Look how he keeps it all to himself. You can't get a hold on the fellow!

He had a mental vision of Maavadiya Pillai sitting at the desk of the new business, the kaasu kadai, and felt a surge of jealousy. But whatever happens, is he likely to acquire the reputation of one who has always been loyal and trustworthy? He will only understand what that is if he stays in one place for forty five years and earns a name. His imagination leapt back over forty five years, and reflected on the direction his life had taken because he had refused to continue at school at that time. Then it had not seemed such a big thing. But later, after his children were born, and various responsibilities attached themselves to his life, the lost opportunity began to look like a huge mistake. He and the Vakil Pillai had been fellow pupils at school. But could he hail him familiarly as "Elé, Arumugam," now?

Pillaiyavargal's mind would not focus on the accounts. He put them away inside the desk. The thought suddenly rose in his mind, The Tuticorin train has not left yet. He muttered to himself, "How long should I beat my breast and carry this corpse?" His forehead broke out in a sweat. He tugged at the desk drawer with unnecessary force. The rupee coins and small change tumbled and scattered. He counted them all, silver, copper and nickel, in great haste. Forty rupees and some smaller coins in all. In a hurry he gathered them up and tied them in a bundle at his waist, put out the light and locked the folding doors.

The bunch of keys were in his hand. Hardly conscious of what he was doing, he walked swiftly towards the station. What had he gained, after all, from forty five years of hard labour? Had he at least eaten a meal he could relish? What, after all, could happen to him? It was only after he had gone some distance that it occurred to him that he had left his slippers behind in the shop.

By some good fortune, he saw no one ahead of him.

So what if they catch sight of me. Must I always go straight home after I've locked up? How is he going to know what's in my thoughts?

He had reached the station. There were sundry railway workers asleep under petromax lamps, porters bandying words in the nearby betel leaf stall. It was a good thing that there wasn't a crowd waiting for the train, thought Pillai, rejoicing secretly.

He placed ten and a quarter annas on the ticket counter and said, "Tuticorin." By this time his mouth was dry.

"Where?" asked the ticket clerk.

Pillai was startled. "Tuticorin," he said again.

"Have you got a kozhukkattai in your mouth or what? Can't you say it clearly?" The clerk punched a ticket and handed it over as he said this.

Appada!

Pillai took a deep breath and let it out slowly like one who has calmed down at last, and entered the platform. The train had arrived and stood waiting. Still another five minutes before it would depart. A soda-water vendor, and a vadai-murukku-poli seller showed off the range of their voices, calling out their wares as they walked up and down the platform. The stationmaster and the railway staff were all congregated by the post and luggage van. He climbed in at the end of the train, into a compartment that was empty of passengers, and sat down by a window facing the goods shed. The stillness outside began to gnaw at him and torment him. He rose, came and sat at a window facing the platform, and gazed in the direction of the engine, eagerly waiting for it to start.

"Pillaivaal! Where are you off to, so late at night," came an imperious voice. None other than his friend Kalyansundaram, who belonged to the railway police. Startled, Pillaiyavargal turned towards him.

A policeman! Pillaiyavargal didn't see his friend, he observed only the khaki uniform.

Without even being aware of what he was doing, he mouthed, "I'm going as far as Tuticorin."

"No hurry! I'll catch up with you at Maniyacchi." And Kalyanasundaram walked off with the measured tread of self-confidence, towards the stationmaster who was standing beside the luggage van.

Minakshisundaram felt a dryness from the tip of his tongue all the way down his throat. His eyes wheeled.

"Colour!, Soda!" called the drinks seller, holding the bottles out.

Pudumaippittan

"Ei, soda! Open a bottle for me," said Pillai.

A hissing sound. "Saar," said the soda seller, holding it out towards him. He gulped it down. Belching loudly, he handed over an anna, then leaned back against the wooden seat and closed his eyes. "Kalyani has seen me now! By tomorrow, everyone will know what I've got up to."

He had a mental vision of Sundaram Pillai waiting for him at the harbour.

The stationmaster's whistle screeched. Pillaiyavargal hurried towards the door of the compartment and clambered down.

The moment he put his foot down on the platform, the train began to move.

"Why have you got off, Pillaivaal?" called a voice from a window, as the train gathered speed and trundled past. Kalyanasundaram, of course.

"They didn't turn up," he shouted back.

Quietly, slowly, Pillai left the station, came out and walked towards the store. It was only after he had gone some way that he remembered that he would never have got on board the ship without a pass. "I ought to be hit with a pair of slippers for my stupidity," he told himself. It was only then that he realized the danger to which he had exposed himself. He began to shake.

He said to himself, "Someone's blessing," took the vibhuti tucked into his waist and placed it on his forehead. "Mahadeva," he said out aloud.

He had arrived at the store. He unlocked the door in his leisurely way and turned on the lights. He took the coins from his waist, replaced them in the desk, then picked up the entry book and wrote, "Minakshi's credit: eleven and a quarter annas." Once again the light was turned off. There was the sound of the slippers as he slid his feet into them, then the click of the lock.

Now his slippers squeaked as he made towards the store manager's house. On the way there, he shook out his upper cloth and re-placed it. He loosened his hair and twisted it up again.

The manager, feeling the need for fresh air, was asleep on the swing.

"Ayya, Ayya," called Minakshisundaram Pillai.

"Why so late, vé" asked the manager, rolling over and yawning.

"Nothing, I had some work to do, that's all. I've put down eleven and a quarter annas to my credit," said Pillai. His mouth was still dry.

"Very well. When you come tomorrow morning at dawn, tell Mukkan to yoke the cart. He's got to go to the market, hasn't he?" Having said this, he put his head down on his folded arm and shut his eyes.

Minakshisundaram Pillai stood there for a while watching the manager. Then he slowly turned round and walked away.

a new nandan

many years passed by since the
untouchable, Nandan, was purified in the fires of Chidambaram,
and turned into a Saivite saint, a Nayanar.

Overcome with pride because of this event, Adanur sank into
a sea of bliss – or sorrow, was it? – and forgot everything.

It didn't even know about the establishment of the British
Empire. Such was its profound sleep.

Now, a number of new signs appeared in Adanur – a railway
station, a stall for betel leaves and nuts, calling itself a Shop,
and a cafe, known as a Hotel. Nobody knew how these matters
came about.

After Nandan said goodbye and left though, there was no
salvation in store for the rest of the paraicheri, the untouchables'

"Pudiya Nandan" was first published in *Manikkodi* in 1934.

settlement. It remained the old street of the untouchables. The same old toddy shop stood there. In modern times, however, the land was leased out by the current priest (descendant of the same priest who officiated in Nandan's times). There was a municipal streetlight at a respectable distance from the cheri, perhaps with the intention of maintaining untouchability. Anyway, nobody knew how to light it. The Paraiyas of the cheri were slaves of the landlord. They were also slaves of the white masters whom they did not know.

The current priest, who was of the very same lineage as the old one (although the chapter describing the history of the clan does not exist in any purana), owned the largest area of land among all the landowners in the agraharam. A thousand veli of land, and so on and so forth. And not only that. Viswanatha Sraudi was a sub registrar with a pension. He had an unswerving faith both in the British Empire, and in the truths of the long dead scriptural rules. Only those people who understood these things, and behaved accordingly, were his devotees.

He had one son, Ramanathan. This son had finished his MA and had been about to take the Civil Service examination to become a Collector. Out of some crazy whim – this at least was the belief of his family and of the agraharam – he became involved in

the Satyagraha Movement. Sraudi believed he could destroy the boy's infatuation for the movement through an appropriate alliance. Such a belief was the result of his own love for his son.

In the cheri, Karuppan was nothing but a walking corpse. He was caretaker and watchman to the big landlord's fields. Something of interest to be noted here. In his youth, either because of his ignorance, or because of Flying too high as the Aiyars say these days, he once climbed into the temple tank, scooped up a handful of water and drank it. That walking representative of God, Subbu Sastrigal, saw this. There was an uproar in the agraharam. Viswanatha Sraudi, then a youth, beat him up so hard, out of such an overwhelming fury, that he blinded Karuppan. You can tell the worth of the growing crop, can't you, by the tip of its blade?

Sraudi had a tender heart, all the same. He pitied Karuppan's desperate condition and gave him the job of caretaker to his fields. He got him married. He built him a hut within the fields. He loved telling everybody that after all this, Karuppan was as good as gold wire.

All this is past history, though.

Just because Karuppan was blind, did it mean he couldn't have children? First there was a boy. His name was Pavadai. The young Saami, the landlord's son, was also born just around this time. When Ramanathan came to the fields occasionally, he would play with Pavadai, both of them diving into the well

---

One of the 63 Saiva saints, **Nandanar,** an untouchable and hence not allowed to enter the temples, longed to see the Lord at Chidambaram, but had to keep deferring the journey. At last he arrived at Chidambaram and circled the walls of the temple, singing and dancing. Siva appeared in his dream and asked him to prepare himself to enter a fire. Nandanar arose from the fire and purified, entered the temple and vanished.

together, or climbing the trees with great enthusiasm, like monkeys.

This too, is past history.

The two boys were to take different steps, leading to different paths in society. They saw the same truth in two different ways.

Now, the Reverend John arrived in Adanur cheri on one occasion, to spread the teaching of Our Father in Heaven. He realized the special nature of Pavadai's intelligence, and tempted Karuppan by saying that if he would allow his son to join the Christian religion, they would help the boy to become as important as a landlord. Anyway, Karuppan was keen that his son should learn Ingurisi. Why go on about it? Pavadai, in short, went off with John Aiyar.

The Reverend John Aiyar was a vellala Christian. At first he put the boy into a boarding school so that he could study there. The boy's intelligence was well recognized, and shone brightly until he reached the tenth class. It might have shone even more. But our Heavenly Father's plans turned out to be different. John Aiyar had a daughter. She was called Mary Lily. A beauty.

She studied along with the boys at the Mission school. Her friendship and affection for Pavadai, (now known as Daniel John) who always gained the first mark in the class, gradually turned into love.

One day, Daniel John, who believed what John Aiyar told him about the lack of cruel Hindu practices within the Christian community, and who therefore allowed himself to entertain fond hopes, went and spoke his mind directly to the Reverend John.

Pudumaippittan

John Aiyar was overcome with rage. "Get out of my house, you paraiya donkey," he said, seizing him by the throat and pushing him out.

For the broken hearted Daniel, the whole world seemed like a wasteland. They say that for people in such a frame of mind, religion is the only means of peace. While he was a Protestant Christian, he had already studied the Bible closely. Now he decided to become a monk, joined the Catholic faith, was accepted as a novice brother to study for the priesthood, and spent two years in a seminary, under the supervision of Father Gnanaprakasam. But eventually, the absurdities that he saw about him, the unnatural desires of some of the priests, and their iron doctrines which brought no peace of mind, served to provoke him into thinking that all their disciplines were nothing but an eyewash and a deceit.

So he said goodbye to that institution too, and became involved in Ramasami Periyar's Self Respect Movement. He became one of the extremists in the movement. Soon he was known as Comrade Narasingam, and began campaigning for his beliefs with an ardour, almost as if he had gone mad.

Once he came to Adanur to visit his father. Perhaps old memories came crowding in. I can't tell you about that. But two truths certainly struck him. One was that there was a huge gulf between him and the rest of his family in terms of thoughts, actions, and in fact in every way. The second was that during the time he had been away, he had acquired a beautiful younger sister – for paraiya women too, have the right to beauty – who was now sixteen years old.

He despaired of there ever being a Bhagirathan who could uplift them and make them aware of themselves as human beings. His own sermons might be heard and understood by the educated. But here, by these speechless insects?

Ramanathan was the favourite of his family. His word was law with them. He studied up to the matriculation examination in the main city of the neighbouring district. His was a different way of studying, though. He was a clever boy, but not only at his studies. Unlike others, he didn't immerse himself in his school work alone. He went along with the flow of the times, engaged with, and took pleasure in, new ideas and feelings.

He went to Chennai to study further, and took an MA. By that time the 1930s Nationalist Movement was under way. He abandoned the prospect of the Collectorship which his father had in mind for him, was beaten up by police batons, and went to jail instead.

As soon as he came out of jail, he joined the Harijan Uplift Movement. Of course his father regretted this. But against Ramanathan's unshakeable resolve, he could only poise his love. His own principles took flight.

Once Ramanathan came to Adanur. At that time, Karuppan's daughter had come of age. Nature had touched her with an absolute grace.

A full moon night. He went into the garden. The night lasted but a few hours. And in Adanur, need you ask? It was even shorter.

A sound as if someone had jumped into the well. He ran to see. There was a woman there, he couldn't tell who. At once he jumped in as well.

"Saami, don't come near me. I'm Karuppan's daughter. I'm just bathing," came a voice.

"All right, all right. I thought you had fallen in. Come out then," he said, climbing out of the well.

"No, saami," she hesitated. What do you think happened next? Nature conquered over both of them, of course.

Later, Ramanathan felt as if he had committed a shocking sin. Karuppan's daughter enjoyed the satisfaction of having received the young landlord's favour.

Ramanathan gave her his word he would marry her. "How can that be, saami," she said, smiling.

He went to Karuppan, told him everything, and asked for his daughter's hand in marriage. But how was Karuppan to understand the new beliefs and rules?

"It would be a terrible sin if that were to happen. I swear by my eyes, you will never, never do it."

Ramanathan felt as if a thunderbolt had hit him.

Mahatma Gandhi came to the south to campaign for the Harijan Movement. He was to stop at Adanur for five minutes. Ramanathan had arranged it all. Sraudigal, ready to dispute with him, was armed with puranic texts as proofs. In such a dispute, Sraudigal believed he would be doubly victorious. First he would demolish Gandhi's policies. Second, he would demonstrate the sanctity of orthodoxy to his son, in the very presence of Gandhi himself.

Comrade Narasingam too arrived in Adanur in order to put some of his own questions to Gandhi. He learnt about his sister's affair. He told his father that she must be married to Ramanathan, that it was certainly possible for them to marry if the paraiya community insisted they should. But he could not shake his father's foolish beliefs. He waited, assuring himself,

"I'll show up the pappaan for what he is!"

There was a raised dais in the grounds next to the railway station. There were gas lights, et cetera, et cetera. A huge crowd. And orthodoxy mingled in the crowd, eager to win.

Old Karuppan longed to look upon Mavaatthuma. Where were his eyes, though? What can one say? What can a blind man do?

He came stumbling along. He thought he heard his son's voice somewhere, and shuffled hurriedly in that direction, thinking that Gandhi had arrived.

Ramanathan, anxious to know whether the garlands had arrived came running along, some distance behind. Meanwhile, Comrade Narasingam too was hastening there, by way of a shortcut.

The Madras Mail comes along jubilantly, wearing its headlight like Siva with his third eye. Adanur is not worthy of its respect. It will not stop. It is rushing past at forty miles per hour.

The engine driver blows his whistle. He screeches his warning. But the blind man continues to walk along the tracks. Has he lost his mind?

Two people have seen him from a distance. His son and – according to Nature's Law, let society say whatever it wants – his son-in-law.

They come running towards him.

Light. Light.

An instant when they all meet. They can almost pull him away.

"Ayyo!"

Pappaan: Derogatory form of addressing or referring to a brahmin.

An arena of blood.

Three people's blood mingled that day. It continues to mingle.

Which of them can we call a Nandan?

Two of them saw a new light. Saw it in two different ways.

Will they be at peace, at least after their death?

They were sacrificed to society. But who thinks of that?

There were big headlines and long columns in the newspapers.

But in Adanur?

ponnagaram

have you heard of ponnagaram,
the golden city? You won't see anything there to compare with
the dreams of the pauranikars, narrators of the puranas. People
speak of merit gained through past deeds. Here, you have to
console yourself by hanging on to that philosophy and its truth.
All the same, for those few human honeybees who are obliged
to live by increasing the profits of a few maharajas of this world,
this is truly a city of gold.

That lane there, look, adjacent to the railway lines, and
leading to the toddy depot, that is its main road. Four people
can walk along comfortably upon it – provided no vehicle comes
towards them. Branching off from it are several bends and curves.
Like rabbit warrens.

"Ponnagaram" was first published in *Manikkodi* in 1934.

Anyone wishing to have a vision of this divine region had best come here when there is a fine rain drizzling and whining, for it is at its unsurpassable best then. Muddy puddles all along the way. Bordering the road, there is the municipal Ganga – or rather, isn't it the Yamuna that is the black river? Beyond that, iron railings. Beyond that again, and at a height, the railway tracks.

On the other side, in rows, human cages. Yes, they are supposed to be dwellings.

Water taps? Yes, there are those. Electric lights? I can't remember. Isn't it enough to light ordinary oil lamps? When there is no moonlight, or when the moon is waning, that is.

The children of Ponnagaram love playing at "Catching fish." But how are fish to be found in the municipality's holy waters? Occasionally an over ripe fruit or a stale vadai or some such thing is likely to come floating down from the homes of the rich. But that is a secret known only to the children of these parts.

Heaven knows what special delight there is in playing by the railway tracks. Of course, there is an iron fence. But can children understand the rule about not going beyond it? And, in any case, if they should Go, the parents are only freed of some of their burden. After all they are not "Glaxo" or "Mellins Food" babies, are they, incapable of squeezing through the railings? It is their special joy to stand in a row chorusing, "Good morni saar" to the product of the iron civilization as it steams past them.

This is by way of their introduction to English education.

The place begins to come alive, and is full of bustle, only after five o'clock. It is from that moment that the women begin their work. Toddy carts arrive, women foregather to collect water. And collecting water there is like taking part in the Mahabharata war.

Hair which started to fade even in youth, and is now as white as spun cotton. Young eyes, ruined. What else can you expect of eyes that watch the mechanical spindles at work day in and day out? Are eyes made of iron? And what about good health and the so-called beauty born of hard work? Good health indeed! Where does that come from? All bacteria, all poisonous viruses, cholera and such-like are produced and cultivated right here. All the same, where there is the will to survive, it will happen, somehow. In ancient stone age times, man lived in a cave, along with lions and tigers. He killed them, they killed him in return. But did he lose his strength, refuse to procreate, become extinct? All life is one great hunt. So what?

A black string around the neck, the symbol of life's commitments. But nobody cares about it much in these parts. It's a different world here, Ayya, the dharmas have to be different, too.

Ammalu is a mill coolie. She can't be more than twenty, twenty two years old. Her husband plies a jutka. He owns this jutka. Five individuals make up the family – Ammalu, her husband Murugesan, his mother, younger brother, and his horse. Their daily meals, including the horse's, depend on the wages of two people. The house rent, the routine bribe to the police, the money for Murugesan's younger brother to smoke ganja on the sly – their wages have to cover all this. They are all occasional tipplers, certainly. How else could they forget their hunger during the Dull season? Hunger, Ayya, hunger! You sing with a great flourish, "All else flies when hunger comes," but the words don't actually touch you. If you were in their position for a single day, those words and their meaning would rise out of your very belly.

That day Murugesan was in great spirits. He and his horse had both drunk their fill and then set out upon a race. The cart turned turtle and its axle broke. The horse was badly wounded. Murugesan suffered severe bruising and internal injuries. When they brought him home he was totally unconscious. It was just as well that he was drunk. At least he wasn't aware of his pain. Ammalu ground up a poultice of sorts and applied it to the swellings. It was then that he muttered something. He wanted some milk kanji, he said. There were two days to go before Ammalu would get her coolie wages. Where was the money?

Ammalu comes to collect water.

It is pitch dark. According to the almanac, there should be a moon tonight, but if it hides behind the clouds, what can the municipality do about it?

There is the usual shouting and screaming. One way and another, the water is collected. She turns to go home.

By the side of the lane lurks a man. He has had his eye on Ammalu for some time.

They both disappear into the darkness. And Ammalu has earned three quarters of a rupee. Yes. So that she can give her husband his milk kanji.

You keep hollering, Chastity, chastity. *This*, ayya, is Ponnagaram.

a murderous gang

dr viswanatha pillai (a mere Licentiate Medical Practitioner), having prepared lists of candidates from the inhabitants of Andhra District for Yama for thirty five years, took his pension and came to live in Azhagiyanambiyapuram. This is a village that lies off the eighth milestone from Palayamkottai, along the Tiruchendur District Board road. (My Tirunelveli friends need not search for Azhagiyanambiyapuram in the district map and tax their brains. It won't be there.)

At about the same time someone else arrived at this village. This was Marudappan, who first served the plantation durais as their barber, gradually acquired the means to run a saloon in the Colombo Fort area, and finally turned himself into the

"Naasakkaara Gumbal" was first published in *Manikkodi* in 1937.

honourable Marudappan Maruttuvanaar, practitioner of herbal medicine, with the help of ten years of profit, and the rote learning of such treatises as *Vakata Shastram*, *Bhogar 200*, and *Korakka Mulikai Chintamani*.

It was entirely by coincidence that these two laid siege to this village at the same time. Yet, after their arrival, a subtle change came over Azhagiyanambiyapuram.

Sri Viswanatha Pillai was born in an ordinary vellala family. He believed that the medical profession would be a profitable one, and took that path from his early youth. It has to be said that the stipend that was offered to those who took up medical studies was a further incentive in this choice. Besides, in those days, a government post was a certainty, if you were a doctor. At the end of the nineteenth century, Western medicine had not made any remarkable progress here. It was a medical science that depended upon an ancient and decayed *Materia Medica* and flowed in a pure stream out of the West and through the channels which were the foreign style hospitals in India. So, it wasn't all that difficult to pass the examination and to find suitable jobs. Besides, the white men were keen only to publicize their own style of medicine.

The story of Sri Viswanatha Pillai's education, his success, and the money he earned, would make an epic, there is no space for it here. But his job of "Cutting corpses" (as it was known) did not turn him into an atheist. He had the same unshakeable faith in the

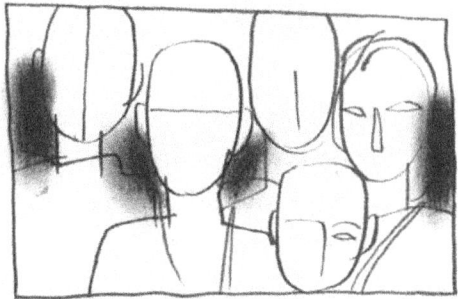

Saiva Siddhanta texts as in *Materia Medica.* During the days when he was employed, the stethoscope and the *Sivagnana Bodham* were of equal significance to him. Besides, such outward symbols as the wearing of vibhuti continued to be important in his life.

In general, Sri Viswanatha Pillai was a good man. He knew how to speak amicably and easily to different people. There was nothing showy about him, no haughtiness because he was a former government employee.

Sri Pillai's family was not a large one. His only son, Mr Krishnaswami was witness to the fact that he had no desire to establish a large and well knit lineage, nor to plant the banner of victory in all eight directions of the world. As for Srimati Viswanatha Pillai (or Salatchi, short for Visalatchi Ammal), the ragi kanji which was all that she ate at midday was evidence that she was a chronic sufferer of a stomach ailment which would not yield to Sri Pillai's outdated treatment. Yet, Salatchiammal filled the house with her bright presence, wearing her sari in the old fashioned manner, with the pleats at the back, and ear ornaments reaching down to her neck.

On his father's insistence, Mr Krishnaswami was in Chennai, trying to put his trust in medical studies, and to follow Sri Viswanatha Pillai's very footsteps.

But the life of Marudappa Maruttuvanaar, practitioner of herbal medicine, did not take a similar course. It saw many more heights and depths. And although his hands toiled until his head grew grey, they were never to be filled with money.

Barber Marudappan took ship from Tuticorin to Colombo in his youth, at a time when neither joy nor sorrow had cast their shadows upon him, when he was full of hope and affection. For the lower caste communities of Tirunelveli, Colombo meant the rubber plantations of Sri Lanka. It was only for the upper caste vellala community that it signified wholesale trade in the Fort area. Marudappan too subscribed to this belief.

He served as barber to the Nuwereliya tea plantation durais, and to the top ranking employees. He received not only plentiful wages, tips and food, but also fell prey to intermittent attacks of malaria. And at last, when he was thirty years old, he set up his own saloon in Colombo. In those days, there wasn't much competition for this kind of work. Many Indians gave him their support and patronage. His career flourished. His one trip to India, and his marriage, were events that just occurred in the midst of all this.

The saloon initiative, besides being a success, also afforded him with the opportunity of acquainting himself with the siddha vaidyam mode of medicine. Besides, in recent times, a Sri Lankan daily, the sacred centre of all discussion among Sri Lankan practitioners of local medicine, became his constant companion, and a means of widening his mind.

When Marudappa Maruttuvanaar got off the train at Tirunelveli station, fifty years old, with all the prestige of one returning from Sri Lanka to his homeland, he brought with him five thousand rupees in cash. Besides, he owned three acres of fertile land in Azhagiyanambiyapuram. He left the saloon in Colombo as a legacy to his son.

Whenever the bus neared Azhgiyanambiyapuram, it was almost as if it proclaimed its arrival with a roll of drums to the eighth milestone which stood on the roadside under a tamarind tree, to Vairavan Pillai's betel leaf stall which stood beside it, to the bamboo gate of Dr Viswanatha Pillai's orchard and grove, and to Marudappa Maruttuvanaar's two storeyed and lime plastered house which stood opposite all this.

On both sides of the road next to the bus stand, there were densely growing tamarind trees. At some time, long ago, a sumaithangi, a structure for resting heavy head loads, had been erected there. How long was it now since the crosswise stone had slipped and fallen away from the uprights? Its right to the name sumaithangi was as tenuous as that of many people who say they belong to a particular religion.

It was the hour of burning midday heat. Even so, not a single ray of light fell on the road. Subbu Pillai, owner of the general grocery store, sat at his cash counter, a book of villuppaatu folk songs dedicated to Sudalaimaadan open on his lap, singing loudly and enthusiastically, to the delight of a couple of men of the maravar community who had spread their upper cloths in the slanting shed in front of the shop, and were seated there, hugging their knees. It was clear when he turned his head with ease and spat out the betel juice that had gathered in his mouth, that it was not just experience but a special skill that he was revealing – for he never interrupted his reading, and neither did his spittle splash the people seated below him, nor did it reach the walls next door. It was Subbu Pillai's secret skill. And the listening maravar, apparently, were completely unaware of it. After all, fame and glory are worshipped only after we build memorials for them. If the maravar knew this philosophic truth, then we can do no more than believe them to be ordinary human beings.

If you go to the land of Malayalam, ei, Sudalai
You'll never return again ...

sang Subbu Pillai.

"By the way, ayya! Have there been people doing black magic in the Malayalam country since the old times?" asked Palavesam Devan, a youth of no great experience. You could forget your hunger as you watched his knotted muscles rolling and sliding when he was at work. He was the son of the village watchman.

"What are you saying? It was in those days that these skills were most widespread. If they could trap Sudalai himself and keep him shut up in a tiny box, can you imagine what else they could do?" This was from Velandi, who came from a different branch of the maravar. His grey hair earned him respect, yet his body had the same firmness that inexperienced youths possessed. He was one of Tamil Nadu's numerous peasants, living avatars of the belief that one can work a small piece of land on a weekly lease, and make a living out of it. He always carried a sickle at his waist. People in the know said its use was not confined to splitting firewood. He was one who always kept his word, always acting according to the belief that it was not fitting for one of the maravar community ever to tell a lie.

Subbu Pillai, overhearing this comment, raised his brass framed spectacles up to his forehead, stared ahead, and then threw in his contribution. "Even the attamma siddhi, the eight supernatural powers, come to us from there. The puranas themselves say so."

In all these matters there was no appeal over Subbu Pillai's judgment, because most Azhagiyanambiyapuram's inhabitants had learnt their first letters by the aid of his cuffs and blows. Nor was Palavesam an exception to this. It was by Subbu Pillai's grace that to this day Palavesam could write his name in crooked letters.

"Then, there was that Kallabiran Pillai who used to live here, blast him! If the man who hawks vessels had not stopped him at his tricks ... I've seen him myself. Our vaidyar knows about it too," said Subbu Pillai, lifting his head and nodding towards the row of houses standing opposite the shop.

It had become his custom, recently, to address Marudappa Maruttuvanaar as vaidyarvaal or doctor, quite unconscious of the fact that the presence of wealth had somewhat lessened his customary caste consciousness.

At this moment the vaidyarvaal was in the front courtyard of his house, burning some green leaves and turning them into ash, blowing at them with a perspiring face. All the same, the conversation half-fell into his snake like ears. Lifting his face and wiping it, he called out, "Pillaivaal, what are you talking about?"

Subbu Pillai called back from the shop, "What was that? Oh, you remember that Kallabiran Pillai who used to live here? I was just talking about him. You knew all about him, didn't you?"

The vaidyar wiped himself, shook out his veshti, refastened it, and made his way towards the shop.

A motor horn sounded in the distance.

"Well, it seems it's one o'clock already. That sounded like the mail bus there! Pillaivaal, have you bathed yet? Shall we go together?" asked the vaidyar, holding on to the railings along the ramp of the shop.

"I was just about to go. Elé, ayya Palavesam, would you mind watching the shop for a while," Subbu Pillai asked, at the same time, looking in the direction of the bus. The passage of the mail bus at one o'clock everyday was an important event in Azhagiyanambiyapuram. There were always some goods for the Shopowner Pillai. As for Doctor Viswanatha Pillai (a member of the Justice Party with its firm beliefs in caste representation in local government, the superiority of Saivism, the Aryan conspiracy, et cetera, but even so ...), his newspaper, *The Hindu*, would arrive. Occasionally, distant travellers who might as well have taken the Trivandrum Express, would arrive by bus instead.

In a couple of minutes the bus had arrived with a tremendous clatter, scattering dry leaves everywhere, and stopped opposite the sumaithangi.

The bus conductor climbed on to the top of the bus, in order to roll down goods and merchandise meant for the shop. The driver got off and strolled towards the shop, to light his bidi. A couple of passengers who had been crouching thus far in the posture of the Vaman avatar, also got out. A couple of paraiya girls with heads shaven in front but plaited at the back, lead hoops stretching their ears down to their shoulders, old chequered saris worn as veshtis around their waists, stood a little apart, carrying baskets full of cowdung and watching the fun.

The conductor who had been throwing down the shop's merchandise, now called out, "Saar, take your suitcase and bedding."

A fashionable youth carrying a wilted newspaper stepped out elegantly from the first class seat next to the driver. His Madras-Broadway fashion plate looks and his foreign style clothes gave him an odd appearance, as if a consecrated idol had somehow slipped from its proper place. Like the old and indifferent bus, his clothes might have been considered old fashioned in London and all the rage in Chennai. But in this world where time could be reckoned in years preceding the birth of Christ, he could only be seen as a man of the future.

Palavesam ran to carry his box, saying, "Edé, it's the Thereserayya's son who has arrived!"

A retired official's son holds a special status in a village at all times! Those whiling away time in the shop immediately gave him that recognition.

"Who is it," asked Velandi, addressing everyone at large, and trying to lever himself up with his hand.

"What, don't you know yet? You know our Theresar Pillai of the West House? It's his son, Maharaja Pillai. Ayya, are you keeping well?" called out Subbu Pillai, from where he sat in the shop.

Maharajan looked in his direction and smiled.

"Yejaman, are you keeping well? Is there much rain in town? Ayya, you look exactly the same as before," said Velandi.

The driver took a couple of pulls at his bidi and threw it away, chewed on some betel leaves, climbed into his seat, and struck his horn with an air that proclaimed, "This bus is about to leave forthwith, passengers should get in." The conductor, who had just remembered, ran as fast as he could to the shop with *The Hindu*.

All the passengers who had been ridding themselves of various bodily discomforts, now came running up. Among them was a Muslim friend, a certain brightness about his face, which gave him the look of a man of influence. He had his eye on the front seat, and came hurrying up, determined to secure it.

The maruttuvar, who had been watching the crowd without a care, smiled at him and began to ask after his welfare. "Well, if it isn't Maraikkayar! What are you doing in these parts?"

The words didn't actually reach Maraikkayar's ears until he had reserved his seat with his upper cloth, climbed into the bus and settled down. Having done that, he held on to the window bars, twisted his whole body so that his pillow slipped to one side, and called out, "Vaidyarvaal! Please come here. There's something I need to tell you urgently. One nimit!"

Marudappa Maruttuvanaar beamed. "What is it, Maraikkayarvaal, what brings you here," he asked, coming up.

"Our Mommad is going to Colombo, I'm just on my way, having seen him off at the isstation. You know Va Ko, don't you, he's offered to take him. Anyway. Didn't you tell me you'd make me a lehiyam? I just thought I'd make sure ... Right now ... Let go of the bus, please. Salaam!" Without allowing the other man to say a word, Maraikkayar Mappilai clinched his business.

"Very well," said the maruttuvanaar. The bus started off in a blast of exhaust fumes.

"Pillaivaal, vaariyala, are you coming," he called out, shaking his upper cloth and tossing it on his shoulder.

"Vaariyala indeed, a vaariyal broom and rubbish to you." Muttering away, Subbu Pillai left his shop and climbed down.

All this while, the decorative puppet stood there, smoking and staring about him in a bewildered way.

"I'll carry the young yejaman's baggage for him, lé, Palavesam, you look after Ayya's shop. Come, yejaman." Velandi made a pad on his head with his upper cloth for the bedding roll, and picking up the leather suitcase, began walking ahead.

The vaidyar and the shopkeeper Pillai pushed open the bamboo gate and disappeared into Dr Viswanatha Pillai's orchard.

The road returned to a lifeless silence. Even the little girls who had been picking up dry twigs disappeared.

Dr Viswanatha Pillai's garden was an extremely pleasant place to be in, during the heat of the day. For those who had been wandering about, perspiring in the heat, the savukkai, or pavilion, which he had built amidst the shade of neem trees and lime groves was a paradise on earth. Except for meal times, Pillaiyavargal would spend his entire time there, in the company of Meikanda Sivachariar. His afternoons were spent with *The Hindu*.

From the path strewn with nandiyavattai and arali flowers where he and the vaidyar were walking, the Shopkeeper Pillai called out, "Ayya, are you there? It looks as if Maharajan has arrived."

Viswanatha Pillai who had been leaning against his easy chair, stooped slightly, and answered, looking over the top of his spectacles, "It's his holidays, he had written to say he would be coming. Where ..." He gathered himself together and rose to his feet.

"Velandi has accompanied him home. Here's your paper. What's the news of the war?" But without waiting for an answer, Subbu Pillai followed the maruttuvar.

In a little while they heard the sound of Viswanatha Pillai closing the bamboo gate.

The lift-well in Viswanatha Pillai's garden was extremely convenient for bathing. You could fill the stone troughs to the brim and stand there, pouring water over yourself all day.

Subbu Pillai tied his upper cloth around his head, put his foot against the washing stone at the base of the well and hitched his veshti up tightly.

The maruttuvar let the water flow out of the half-full stone trough and began to wash it out. Then he said, "Ayya, I wanted to ask you something ... You know the field by the pond which yields three marakkal's worth, there is some talk that it is going up for sale. You know the one I mean, to the west of our pannai pillai's boundary. Our lad Mukkam came to me the other day. I listened to what he said, and I thought that if I bought it, it would work out to my advantage. What do you say?"

With a hissing sound, Subbu Pillai poured the first bucket of water into the stone trough, and then lowered it into the well once more. It filled with water. He looked up and into the vaidyar's eyes.

"Vé! Why do you want to go and annoy these important people? This is a matter only for the big men. Haven't you seen what that Mukkam lad had to go through? Didn't you see that the pannaiyar pretty nearly tortured him? Maybe the pannaiyar has an eye on the land himself. Leave the wretched business alone."

"What are you saying, ayya? If he has wealth, that's his business. Just because he's a pannaiyar, does he have to plant his personal flag over everything? Must we leave well alone whenever we see his flag? I'm not scared of him. I'll finish the business tomorrow. Let's see what happens." Marudappan spoke in anger.

'Well, I've spoken my mind. You must do as you wish," answered Pillai.

It was evening, daylight had faded. Only the radiance of the western skies and the sudden rustling of palm fronds in the just-awakened evening breeze, signified that the sun's work was done.

Subbu Pillai walked along the road towards the west of the lake, a cloth tied about his head, a couple of palm fronds in his hands. A cart yoked to a couple of bullocks descended from the cart track that joined the road from the eastern shore, the lively noise of the cartman mingling with and resounding against the jingling of bells and the rasping of wheels against the loose gravel.

Even though the light was dim, the sound of Thoplaan's voice made it clear that the cart was the pannaiyar's.

Subbu Pillai, who had stepped to one side, called out, "What, Annacchi, returning home in the dark, are you? Where have you been?"

Pannaiyar Chidambaram Pillai, who had been resting against a bolster in the cart, called out the order, "Edé, stop the cart," and it came to a standstill in a little while.

Chidambaram Pillai threw his slippers out on the road, gently eased his feet into them and climbed out.

"You know Meyinna of Kilanattam?"

"Oh yes, he's our Na Ko's wife's brother, isn't he?"

"The same fellow. His wife had a sister who was married in Marundur. She died suddenly. I'm just returning from the sixteenth day rites."

"But didn't madani go with you?'

"Is she likely to have stayed home? Of course she came with me. There's no one to give them a hand there. She said she'd stay on for a bit. I've left her there with them. After all she has nothing much to do at home."

"Yes, why not ... How old would that lady have been?"

"She wasn't all that old. Might have been about thirty."

"Were there any children? Anyway ... Annacchi, I've been thinking that I must tell you about something. I just happened to hear about this. I feel it wouldn't be right if I didn't tell you," said Subbu Pillai.

The pannaiyar, afraid that he was making overtures in order to borrow money, stepped towards the lake, saying, "Have you done your evening observances?"

He left his slippers on the lake shore, walked into the water and began splashing his face and legs amidst loud growls and sounds of "Om."

Subbu Pillai, who had finished his evening rituals and worship, although perfunctorily, now sat quietly on the stone slab used for washing clothes, waiting for the pannaiyar to finish.

The pannaiyar touched his forehead with vibhuti, repeated from memory the Tirumurugar-attrupadai and a couple of verses from Tiruvasagam, called out "Siva," and returned ashore.

"You know our Marudappan. He earned a paisa or two in Colombo, and that has gone to his head. Today, when we were bathing at the new Theresar Pillai's well, he said, "The pannaiyar can keep his wealth. Does he think he can fly his flag over the whole village or what?" He said he's prepared for a trial of strength. Just see what this village has come to!"

"If the creature wants to bark, let it. He's become a maruttuvar, so he's got to show off. Anyway, what is it all about?"

"You know that Mukkuruni visam, yielding three marakkals, which is next to your fields. That fellow Mukkam's land. It's all to do with that. Marudappan is boasting he wants to buy it."

"Mukkam's land? Didn't he fall at my feet and plead with me to buy it just the other day? I drove him off because I didn't want to help the ungrateful dog. I suppose he went and fell at this man's feet. All this boasting for just that!"

"I said to him, why do you want this land, da, it's only appropriate for the pillai community. That was it. He ranted away that all the pillais of this village are like this, we're all violent and obstinate, and that he's not going to give in."

"Is that so? Elé Thoplaan! We are going to walk home. You go on with the cart, untie the bullocks, and then bring that Mukkam to me, however late it is."

"You mustn't let it be known that you bought the land yourself. After all, the Theresar also expresses a wish ... Do it in his name."

"Why should I? If I fling in a few extra coins, it should do it. Why should I lie to that dog?"

"No, no, Annacchi, you don't know. Please listen to me."

"Come to my house after you've locked up the shop for the night. We'll talk about it then."

"Appa, what is the matter with Amma? Her health hasn't improved at all. You aren't looking after her properly, it seems," said Maharajan.

A moth collided against the hurricane lamp which stood opposite them. He turned up the wick which was beginning to dim.

"Is it in our hands? There can't be a medicine that we haven't tried these past twenty years." Viswanatha Pillai removed his spectacles and rubbed his eyes.

"Because you started taking your pension, has medicine itself decided to take a pension from you? How can you talk like this?"

"What can I say? I've spoken the truth. Her intestines have become weak. Nothing I give her seems to suit her constitution."

"May I try a particular course on her? It follows Natural Medicine. First she must fast for a while. Then there'll be a crisis. If we begin the treatment after that, it is likely to be successful."

'What is the matter with you, da. You're supposed to be at a Medical School. How did you come upon Natural Medicine? Don't waste your time and then fail your exams."

"I'm certainly studying for that too. But this course has really cured many patients. I've administered it myself."

"Very well, try it then. I'm not saying you shouldn't."

As they spoke, they heard the sound of slippers outside the savukkai. And then, while Thoplaan stood outside, holding a hurricane lamp, the pannaiyar and Subbu Pillai stepped into the light within the savukkai.

"Why, it's the pannaiyar! What brings you here, in the dark? Come you must sit here in this chair. Subbu Pillai, please take the bench. What brings you here, at this late hour?" Viswanatha Pillai stood up with ostentatious courtesy.

"No particular business. I happened to be in these parts, so I thought I would look in on you, at least. So, mappilai, how come you are here, are you on leave?"' Pannaiyar took a special delight in calling the young man son-in-law.

"Yes, it's the summer vacation, he arrived this afternoon. Raja, why don't you go to the shop and buy a packet of scented tobacco?" As he said this, Viswanatha Pillai arranged some betel leaves on their silver salver.

Subbu Pillai and Chidambaram Pillai spoke together,

"But I shut up shop long ago ..."

"Are you taking all that trouble just for me? But shop tobacco never agreed with me in any case. Elé, Thoplaan, why don't you bring me my betel leaf container? What are you staring like that for?"

Maharajan, who had just begun to set off, sat down once more, leaning against a pillar.

Chidambaram Pillai stretched out his head into the dark to spit, and then said, "There's no air even in this savukkai, of course people will just roast in the village. Annacchi, how is the crop this year?'

"Hardly any yield to speak of. Whatever well water there is, just gets poured and dries at the roots."

"Maybe you should plant some ten to thirty rose bushes and let them flower, all you have to do is to get a small lad to look after them ..." said Chidambaram Pillai. Then, tiring of this conversation, he looked at Subbu Pillai pointedly.

"Theresar Pillaivaal, I wanted to ask your advice on a particular matter. Ayya just accompanied me. It's to do with this village ... There are some fellows who are going about with swollen heads. Just come this way ..." Subbu Pillai took Viswanatha Pillai outside.

"Yes, yes, how true ... It's between the buyer and the seller, what do we care ... Oh, is that so? So he interfered in Pillaivaal's business, did he? ... I knew ages ago ... If he builds a brick house, does he become blind as well?" Viswanatha Pillai's words came intermittently, falling here and there.

After a few minutes, the two men returned to the savukkai.

"Well ..." smiled the pannaiyar.

"Why should you come all this way, just for such a small thing? If you had told me, wouldn't I have come to you instead? Raja, please run home and bring me the keys which I've left in the glass almirah. Take this tonic for your mother at the same time and give it to her. We'll start on the course you prescribe tomorrow."

Raja shook out his upper cloth, placed it on his shoulder, and went out.

"How is she, at home? Not too bad, I hope. How many more years does our mappilai have to study? Shouldn't we finish off the marriage in good time?"

"I think so too. He finishes his studies next year. My wish is to hold the marriage during the month of Thai, next year. Why isn't there any sign of Mukkam yet?" Viswanatha Pillai turned his head, hoping to hear voices outside.

"Wretched fellow will turn up soon. We must sign the document tonight. Tomorrow we can register it in town. Once all the hullabaloo has died down, it can be transferred to my name."

"Doesn't he know all that? We just need to finish the business now," said Subbu Pillai.

Four or five days later. The afternoon heat stung, almost peeling the skin off one's back.

Marudappanaar gathered handfuls of herbs and green leaves which were scattered about in fields and woods, but which only he knew about, then walked along the road above the lake and climbed down the steeply sloping stone steps to rinse them in the water. The upper cloth which he had been wearing as a hood kept slipping down, preventing him from bending down to his work, so he stood up again, removed it from his head, tied it tightly round his waist and stooped down once more.

A voice came to him from the maruda tree. "Vaidyarayya, it seems that at dead of night Theresar Pillaivaal swooped down on Mukkam's land and made off with it."

He looked up. Velandi was chopping down leaves from a maruda tree, for the goats waiting down below.

"What if the vellalas of the village gang up? If there is a time for the elephant, there will come a time for the cat too. So, it seems the pannai pillai wasn't content until he got his own hands on that piece of land. I thought, if I bought it, it would be of advantage to me. Forget those wretched men's words."

"By the way, it seems Mukkam has set off for Colombo ... Why was the fellow in such a hurry to take the money and run?"

"Let the mudhi get lost. I was sorry for him when he came to me and wept like that. If people who bear the community name Devar hide away and keep as quiet as cats, then anything can happen in this village ... Does it belong only to the pillais, or what? In that case, all of us should get out. Let them try and prevent us," said the vaidyar. Then he called out, "Dé, Thoplaan, what's the hurry, where are you off to?"

Thoplaan came running along at top speed. "Oh, is this where you are? Theresarayya's wife is in a terrible condition, they wanted me to call you. But has the town bus gone already? Did you see it?" He stared in the direction from which the bus was expected, as he asked this.

Pudumaippittan

"Oh, is that how it is? Is it possible to tie up the wind? Velandi, remember what I said about a certain matter. Just you watch."

The maruttuvanaar tied up his dripping leaves and set off towards the village, by the shortcut.

"Well, Thoplaan, where are you going?" asked Velandi.

"I'm not off anywhere. But the yejaman from Chennai is going to town to fetch a big daakkutaar."

And just then, Maharajan came by, his care worn face bereft of its Madras lustre. "What, da, has the bus arrived yet?" he asked.

"No yejaman, nothing has turned up yet," replied Thoplaan.

At about twelve o'clock that night Srimati Viswanatha Pillai – Salatchi Achchi – died. Need you ask about the elaborate funeral customs in a village? From that hour there was incessant weeping and wailing in the house.

Viswanatha Pillai sat on a bench outside, his head bowed low. Maharajan leaned against a pillar, looking down and pulling at his fingernails. Chidambaram Pillai too was there, on the outside bench, inseparable from his betel nut box, talking to the people who had come to offer their condolences, and ordering the servants and Subbu Pillai as they went about their work.

Although Salatchiammal's body had been enfeebled, it would not have collapsed if Maharajan's Nature treatment had not been embarked upon.

He began his initial treatment, expecting there to be a crisis. At a time when the disease itself was giving her an aversion to any kind of food, a total fast weakened her disastrously. Just two days of fasting, and her pulse was barely there.

When she was in this state, Marudappa Maruttuvanaar was summoned. He felt her pulse and then gave his opinion, "We can only say anything with certainty after forty eight naazhigai. Until then you must keep her warm with continuous hot compresses of bran." And so he left. The doctor who arrived at eight gave her a couple of injections which gave her a troubled clarity for a brief hour. In the end her spirit departed, with a single yearning, "I wasn't fortunate enough to see my son married to the pannaiyar pillai's daughter."

"Elé Thoplaan, why hasn't the barber showed up, lé? Did you look for him?" scolded Chidambaram Pillai.

"Yes, I found him at home. He told me, "You go ahead, I'll be there immediately," said Thoplaan.

"What does he mean, he'll come later? It's already two hours. You go and give him another shout."

Palavesam dragged in a couple of coconut fronds, dropped them with a thud and said, "Are you asking after Madasami? I just saw him walking towards the vaidyar's house."

"Go there and bring him immediately. See how late it is," said Chidambaram Pillai.

A quarter of an hour later, Palavesam returned on his own. But he came at a run. "Yejaman, I went there, sure enough. Madasami was standing outside. He told me, Hereafter, this barber won't be available for this kind of thing, it is not his real work."

Subbu Pillai, who had been weaving the coconut fronds into small mats, asked, "Were those Madasami's words?" and rose to his feet.

The **barber** plays a significant role at funerals, making the announcement, and shaving the mourners. The funeral cannot take place without him.

Pudumaippittan

"No, it was Marudappan who said that."

"He actually said that, and you listened quietly and came away to report it? Aren't you a maravan? Couldn't you have given him a couple of blows on the snout and dragged him here? And Velandi, why are you standing here, doing nothing? Drag those whoresons here with their hands tied behind their backs. I'll flay the skin off them," roared Chidambaram Pillai.

Viswanatha Pillai tried to make peace. "Wait, Annacchi. He's shirking his duty because he wants a few extra coppers. Why don't we just fling them to him?"

Chidambaram Pillai roared once more, "You don't know the customs of this village. You don't seem to realize that he has to do his duty as a barber. Elé, Thoplaan go and cut down a good, stout tamarind cane for me."

Within another half-hour, the result of Chidambaram Pillai's Sugriva-style command could be seen in the procession coming towards Viswanatha Pillai's house, accompanied by a frightful noise.

Velandi shoved Madasami and Marudappan forward by their necks. He had tied their arms to each other's behind their backs.

"If you turn around, I'll slice off your heads with my sickle. Walk on, what are you staring for?" The voice of authority could be heard above the wailing of the barber's family who followed behind, weeping and striking themselves on the stomach.

"Tie up both the fellows to that post over there. Well, Madasami, are you going to see to your work, or do you want some more?" asked Chidambaram Pillai.

"I can't, Ayya," muttered Madasami.

Even the women who had been indoors, mourning, now came outside to watch the racket.

"Where's the cane, da?" He picked up one of the canes, and used it repeatedly on Madasami's back and legs. Unable to bear the pain, he started screaming and shouting.

From the howls his wife was raising, it became apparent to everyone present that it was Marudappan who had encouraged Madasami's conduct.

Now Marudappan spoke up. "Do you think that because you are pillais, you have sprouted horns on your heads? Is this the British Rajyam, or isn't it? So you are prepared to throw your weight about, are you? Do you think you can just tie up a man and beat him up, as if there isn't such a thing as justice? People who laugh today should also consider what's in store for them tomorrow."

"He doesn't seem to know his place as a barber, Velandi. Prise his kneecap off and hand it to him. Give it to him good and proper until this other fellow is prepared to take up the conch. Come on, why are you just standing there!"

Velandi lifted up his staff and brought it down with a tremendous crack on Marudappan's knees. The vaidyar screamed with pain, "Ayyo! Amma! They have killed me. Is there no justice in this village! Is there no law!"

Viswanatha Pillai came running outside and plucked the staff out of Velandi's hand saying, "Annacchi, I can't bear to watch this. You must think about what you are doing. Let the wretched fellow go. Her fate turned out like this. And that's the reason why these men's wits have turned."

Velandi gave yet another blow, saying, "See what my fist is like, lé." Marudappan's two front teeth fell out.

Shocked out of his wits by the sight of blood, tears filling his eyes, Madasami began to blow the conch.

"Untie the wretch, da. If I ever see you in these parts again, I'll cut off one leg and the opposite arm, Now run off, dog," shouted Chidambaram Pillai.

Marudappan, having been untied, hopped off, supported by his wife. At a distance, he took a handful of earth and threw it up to the skies, calling out in anger and frustration, "One day, you too will end up like this burning dust. One day, you too will end up with the pain that I feel now."

By the time they finished the funeral rites one way and another, it was four o'clock.

It came to Chidambaram Pillai's knowledge that Madasami had put up with his backache because of a small loan that Marudappan made to him with a certain instruction, "Either you return this money to me, or do as I say." But Chidambaram Pillai was not bothered by all that.

He sent a warning to Marudappan through Velandi, "If this reaches the ears of the police-gilice, your head won't be safe on your shoulders." Then at last he began to console and comfort Viswanatha Pillai.

Viswanatha Pillai was in a panic, what with the loss of his wife, the funeral rites which had turned into such a shambles, and his knowledge, dating from the days of his employment, of the extent of the local government's authority.

During their many conversations, Viswanatha Pillai also mentioned his wife's last wish. "We'll finalize it, just as you said, during the month of Thai," the pannaiyar said, bringing that matter to a conclusion.

After Marudappan went home and lay down that evening,

he never came out again, because of his humilation, his raging frustration, and quite simply, the sheer violence of the blows he experienced.

Secretly, without anyone knowing, he sent a complaint to the Srivaikundam Police Station. The messenger was warned and driven off, the complaint rejected. When the whole village ganged up against one, what use was money? Anyway, he came from a community that was considered low, who engaged in work that was held in contempt. At times a huge rage filled him and he wanted to destroy the whole village. At other times he felt an endless weariness.

News of these events spread to the neighbouring villages, whispered half-truths and three-quarter-rumours. The vellalas swelled out their chests. Many people arrived post haste, and with evil intent, to give free advice, "Keep these fellows well under control, otherwise we'll make sure that other barbers from the Malayalam state are brought and installed here as they have been elsewhere."

Maharajan could hardly bear to stay in Azhagiyanambiyapuram. He longed for the sixteenth day observances to be over and done with, so that he could return to Chennai.

While things were in this state, the news was put about that Marudappan had gone missing. This was a shock to the entire village. The house was locked and shut up. It was a wonder how he could have left, and where he could have gone.

Chidambaram Pillai didn't bother himself with this news either. He had considerable satisfaction in the thought, "The wretch was terrified of me, and ran off to Colombo."

Nowadays, Viswanatha Pillai found it difficult to go home

even to eat his meals. Maharajan himself would bring him his food, at appropriate times, to the savukkai. Maharajan thought to himself, "How can I leave Appa here, on his own? Why shouldn't he come with me?" But Pillai, who loved his savukkai, refused to do so. Pillai and pannaiyar grew very close. They were seldom apart. The Doctor acquired an unshakeable faith in Chidambaram Pillai's ruffianly daring. As for Chidambaram Pillai, he had the ruffian's affection for the doctor's blind and childlike innocence.

Subbu Pillai's thoughts, however, took a new turn. He realized the truth that it was a desire to possess more land that caused the entire catastrophe. He whispered into Viswanatha Pillai's ears. The words fell sharply upon that devastated heart and took root there. Slowly hatred began to grow within Viswanatha Pillai, unknown to himself, still afraid to reveal itself. All the same, Subbu Pillai began to fantasize that he might get his daughter married to the doctor, as his second wife. A certain amount of money would come in. With luck, this dog's life would come to an end.

The sixteenth day rites were over. Subbu Pillai chose his moment carefully and planted his seed. Now all he had to do was to nourish it. It was his profound belief that it would sprout on its own.

A simple, private marriage would do!

Five days had passed since the sixteenth day rites. Maharajan stood waiting for the bus with a shaven head. His father, the pannaiyar pillai and Subbu Pillai stood next to him.

The bus came to a standstill. A passenger climbed down in the dark.

Maharajan climbed in. His luggage was carried up. The bus started.

"Drop me a line as soon as you arrive," called out Viswanatha Pillai.

"Oh, is that Theresar Pillai? Who's leaving on the bus?" came a voice.

"Maraikkayarvaal? What brings you here?"

"I came to see the pannaiyarvaal. Of course, there he is. You know the land you bought from Mukkam, it was already mortgaged to me. I just came to inform you about this. And our vaidyar and his wife converted to Islam yesterday. They are on this very bus, on their way to Colombo. He is going to be the manager of my shop there," said Maraikkayar.

"There is a court. We'll see what happens there," replied Chidambaram Pillai.

a well of sorrows

if you were to mention the place-name Vasavanpatti, the inhabitants of Tirunelveli district themselves would not recognize it. Even if you were to scrutinize a map of the area you would not be aware of its existence. It is a tiny hamlet which is not considered worthy of that honour. Palmyra trees surround the village. The District Board road, symbol of the imperialism of petrol culture, also seems to think the village beneath its notice, and runs half a mile away from it. If you leave this main road and walk about a mile along a cart track bordered by thorn bushes and cactus, you will arrive at a palmyra grove. Any footpath appearing within the grove will most certainly bring you to the boundary of Vasavanpatti.

The first indication that you are in the village is the sudden

---

"Thunbakeni" was first published in *Mannikkodi* in 1935.

end of the palmyra grove, and the miraculous reappearance of the cart track, between broken down walls. Those walls, standing directly opposite each other, surround two Nandavanam, the pleasure gardens. Golden and red arali and wild malli grow without restraint in those enclosed spaces. Within each nandavanam there is a well.

Having crossed these, you come to the east facing temple, in its current state of decoration, greatly ruined, with broken walls, empty of its gopuram. The agraharam is no more than two or three houses whose roofs have fallen in, besides the priest's house. Twenty feet away the cart track turns once more, passes between cactus and yellow flowering portia trees, and becomes the street of the pillais. The big house roofed with flat tiles, finished off with curving tiles along its lower slopes, belongs to the landowner, Nallakkutraalam Pillai. Further on, between two or three curves of the track lie the cottages belonging in turn to the

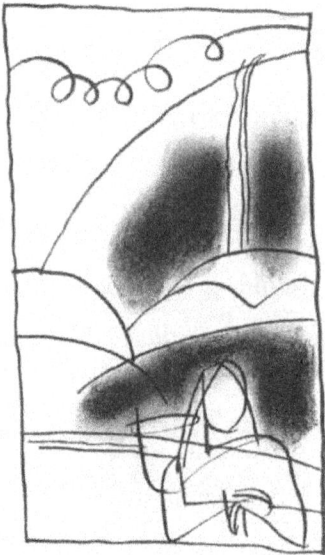

Accountant Mudaliar, then to Ki Mu Sankaralingam Pillai, to the grocery shopowner Ottappidaaram Pillai, Ottappidaaram was his ancestral village, to the teacher, Subbu Pillai, and to the pusari serving at the Pillayar temple, Venalingam Pandaram. A glimpse of the other cottages will tell you that they do not possess all those conveniences of daily living that the landowner, the pannaiyar pillai takes for granted. For these are all people who earn their livelihood by cultivating the pannaiyar's lands

Pudumaippittan

on some kind of tenancy arrangement. All the vellalas formed a group, loyal to each other.

Once you cross this street, perfumed with the pungent smell of coconut oil, you will come to a waste ground. In the midst of that, like a lone king of the forest, or a radiant light burning in the cremation ground, the guardian deity of the village, Sudalaimaadan Peruman's shrine stands, firm and strong, like a giant tree, built of bricks and plaster. He is held in greater honour by the villagers than Mahavishnu, who manifests himself in the idol of the broken down temple. Did Sudalaimaadan know of this perhaps? Around the shrine, there are five or six huts belonging to the maravar. The village watchman lives there, among others. Beyond these huts there is the Manamaari lake, looking up to the heavens for water. Towards the right of its nearest shore is the cheri where the low caste community live. There are perhaps some thirty huts there.

In the street of the vellalas, farmers, close to the waste ground, and just opposite Ottappidaaram Pillai's grocery shop, there is a savukkai, an open shelter built by the pannaiyar pillai, like a pavilion with a palmyra frond roof. Village gossip, Ki Mu's administration, dice games, all these took place there. Rush mats, dirty pillows and bolsters were left scattered about in various corners, to be used by people who slept there on summer nights, or for the Big men to relax and lean against during the day.

You could buy everything at Ottappidaaram Pillai's store, from Ruler cigarettes to hair oil. On occasions such as Sivaratri, or during the offering to Sudalaimaadan, he would even sell playing cards. But Ottappidaaram Pillai was not one to conduct business in groceries alone. In primary education matters such as alphabet books and multiplication tables, he was capable of engaging in the bartering of goods. When the inspiration came upon him, he read and recited from folk tales such as Alliarasaani Maalai and Marudai Veeran Kathai to the Tevar community assembled in front of his shop. If he chanced to overhear animated discussions going on in the savukkai, he made his contribution to it, without even leaving his shop.

Once the summer season was in full swing – and better still, when the harvest was in progress – Ottappidaaram Pillai made a killing, while Isaakki Nadar who ran a toddy shop next to the cheri fared even better. From five in the afternoon until ten or eleven at night, the racket in front of Pillai's shop exceeded that of a marketplace.

The summer harvest had begun at Vasavanpatti. It was evening, just about sunset time. The accountant and Ki Mu were sitting together in the savukkai. Ki Mu was deeply engrossed in sorting out the taxes owed. In front of him were laid out the government note books, brown with age, a long bag, et cetera et cetera. The watchman, Kattayyappa Tevan, stood by, against the outer edge of the savukkai.

Thitharappa Mudaliar, the accountant, called out to him, "Kattayyappa, get me some lime paste, please. And it looks as if the betel nuts are all finished too. Get me a duttu's worth of each, won't you?"

"Yes, buy what he wants, and then look for that Vellayyan and drag him here. He's always like this. I have to set off for the cutchery at crack of dawn tomorrow. Now is that everything?" Ki Mu Pillai was transferring all his accounts into his ledger.

Just at that time, the pannaiyar pillai walked up, covered in the dust and chaff of the field, his umbrella held against his side, followed by two or three maravars who listened to his words respectfully, arms folded. He came into the savukkai, hot, sweating, and sat down with a sigh, "Appada."

"Come and sit down, Annacchi. Are you in good health?" Ki Mu asked.

"Good health? Nonsense! Leave it alone. Ei, Aandi! Just run up to the house and check if they need anything," said the pannaiyar, ordering off one of his men.

"Well, Annacchi, it seems you've begun harvesting the Aladi fields? Wait, you clod! Can't you see I'm talking to Annacchi? ... These low caste donkeys are really getting above themselves these days." Ottappidaaram Pillai reprimanded a small girl and began engaging the pannaiyar in conversation.

"Oh there's no shortage of anything. Certainly not of problems. On Monday, last week, I went to court. It seems they are heaping up imported rice by the sackful, Pettai Pillai told me. As for this place, even if you wrestle with the earth you hardly get anything. Is that Marudi standing there? Ei, mudhi, go and throw a couple of handfuls of straw into the cattleshed, and then come back here." Having demonstrated his authority, he said to Ottappidaaram Pillai once more, "Pillaivaal, if my servant turns up here, tell him to follow me to the nandavanam." Then he set off again, taking a shortcut.

The shopkeeper chatted to Marudi. "Well, di, they say your husband owes money and that the pannaiyar is furious about it. Of all things, should you go and make enemies of big men, di?"

"What saami, my pallan only borrowed some two hundred from the pannai yejaman, saami. If even big men and elders of the village treat us like this, what can we do, saami? And what if he bought two bullocks and a cart? And now even those ... Sudalai alone must look after us! If these people insist like this, where are we to go for the money, saami? Saami, just give me this lump of jaggery, and this tobacco, and these withered betel leaves. I'll just go and see to the cattleshed." Marudi poured out her tale of woe and then went off to work.

When Marudi's husband took a loan from the pannaiyar, it cannot be said for certain that he did so in the belief that he would return it. He probably did so in the hope that he might put the animals to use for a bit, and then, when they grew tired and weak, he'd cast himself at the yejaman's feet, and get by without returning his debt in cash. But this pannaiyar was not the sort to give in to any amount of servile begging and pleading. Besides, what could the pannaiyar pillai do? Everywhere there was a shortfall, he might not even be able to pay his taxes. Afraid that the government would confiscate his land, he acted harshly towards those individuals with whom he would normally have been more lenient. He confiscated the bullocks. That was the last straw. There was a furore in the village cheri. Vellayyan and his wife shouted themselves hoarse. For some time Vellayyan protested strongly. He was beaten up for his pains.

The pannaiyar complained in disgust about his labourers. He was embittered by their lack of gratitude, however much he did for them.

And that night Vellayyan didn't go home till very late.

The next day, early in the morning, the pannaiyar thought he might just take a glance at his cattleshed before setting out. There were only Vellayyan's old bullocks there, chewing cud and rising to their feet when they heard human footsteps. His own well bred greys weren't to be seen. At once he woke up Ki Mu Pillai and showed him the empty cattleshed. Then they both aroused the Talaiyaari Tevan who was asleep by the savukkai and told him everything.

Talaiyaari Tevan immediately suspected Vellayyan. When he went to investigate, only Marudi was in the house. When she saw the three men there, and when they enquired where her husband was, she immediately lied that he had been there all the time and had only just set out.

Talaiyaari Tevan knew only one way of ascertaining whether what she had just said was true or false. He caught her by the hair immediately, flung her to the ground and began kicking her. Tevan got a special pleasure in doing that.

However much she shouted and screamed, Talaiyaari Tevan would not give in. By this time, crowds had gathered in the cheri, the slum. News of the theft spread like wild fire. Many reported that they had seen Vellayyan in the toddy shop, late into the night.

And then? All Marudi's shouting and screaming came to nothing. They came upon Vellayyan dead drunk and dead to the world, in the palmyra grove. Once he was caught, what did it matter, whether he had actually committed the theft or not? The matter was very soon turned over to the police, and Vellayyan was sent to jail.

Until he was actually sent to jail, the village was in a fine commotion. There were plenty of matters to discuss tirelessly, endlessly. However hard the pannaiyar hit, there was no sign of his bullocks. Did that mean he should allow this fellow, Vellayyan, to get off scot free? His contention was that he should spend a spell in jail at least for making off with his money.

During this chaotic time, Marudi was two months pregnant. As far as she was concerned, given the conditions in the cheri, life was sweet when she first married Vellayyan. If, in the first pride of being a new bridegroom, he had gone and bought the bullocks and cart, how could he have known then, how it would all end? And what was she to do about it now? Of course she was inordinately fond of Vellayyan. Even though they had got drunk together and quarrelled frequently, the evil eye of the cheri must have fallen upon them. Anyway, Vellayyan went to prison. Marudi went home to her father's house. All that the pannaiyar could do was to shout abuse. All the same Vellayyan's imprisonment recompensed him in some way for the money he had lost.

At a time of drought, when the land was scorched and everyone suffered from poverty, what more could one hope for, even in one's own father's house, other than love and concern? And when one is no more than a poor paraiya? Just at that time, though, there was a scheme to gravel the main road. Marudi and her parents found some sort of employment for two or three months, and had a little money in hand. There was no anxiety at home, except for the fact that her husband had been jailed unfairly.

But can the District Board be so crazy as to go on gravelling the roads forever? Once again they were caught within the cycle of poverty and want.

Then an agent, eager to recruit labourers for a tea plantation, turned up. From the perspective of the cheri, life on a tea plantation seemed like heaven on earth. They say you should even cross the ocean in search of wealth. So what if you crossed

Pudumaippittan

the ocean and staked your very freedom? At least at the end, there might be a sum of money to bring home.

Marudi and her mother set off with the kangaani, the agent, for Colombo.

Viswamitra and Vyasa, those ancient seers, went up the mountain for a particular reason. Mr Stoddart, ICS, went to his mountain for quite a different one, and it has to be said that if Srimati Marudi Ammal took to the mountains in her turn, she had her reason too. They say it isn't polite to enquire too closely into the purvasrama of the sages, their life before they became monks. It should be the same, in regard to Marudi Ammal's sojourn in the mountain.

It was the firm belief of the present owner of the Crown Tea Estates, Sir Joseph Fitzmartin Crown, that Waterfalls had been placed by god in Sri Lanka for the specific purpose of creating a tea plantation. The interesting thing about this is that Sir Joseph had never left the shores of England. Apparently, a certain medical expert of Harley Street who attended on the family, had assured him that a country where English beef and English bacon were not subject to that doctor's inspection, would not suit Sir Joseph's health. So it was Sir Joseph's custom to leave the management of his tea estates to those individuals who were prepared to give themselves up to heat and malaria, in return for two thousand pounds a year.

At present, Patrickson Smith was the forty five year old bachelor who had taken up the management of Waterfalls. There were two matters which he understood clearly. One was the meaning of bachelorhood in the context of a tea estate, the other was the code of behaviour towards black people in the context of tea cultivation. As well as this, he could speak the language of the black coolies fluently.

Among the black coolies, Waterfalls was known as Vaaterpaalam, the water bridge. It got its name because of its location on the slopes of the Sri Lankan hills, next to a waterfall. The tea estate, two miles long and three miles wide, stretched along both sides of the waterfall. The white gentleman's bungalow had been built above the waterfall, along a pathway. In front, and on the opposite shore of the nameless forest stream, were the coolies huts, like chicken coops. Some distance away, were a hospital and the dwellings of the black overseers. As for these sub managers, except for the colour of their skin, in every other aspect they had the mental disposition of the durais, the white men. If you were to go and live there, you could develop only two sorts of mental attitudes. One turned you into a black durai, the other prepared you for prison. Yes, there was a third possibility too. To put a fullstop to your life.

From the time they stopped at Thattappaarai, took ship and arrived at the mountainside, Marudi and her mother were as keen as if they were about to dig up a buried treasure. As soon as they arrived at Vaaterpaalam, they were delighted by the seasonable cool weather and by the quarters that were assigned to them. Blankets to cover themselves against the cold at night and rain during the day when they plucked the tea leaves, wages in hand every week! Everything seemed comfortable. The stench was somewhat greater than they had known in Vasavanpatti cheri. But they got used to that too, in a few days. Because it was bitterly cold, they would wake up only at seven in the morning. After that, they would cook some kanji and eat it, sling

Pudumaippittan

a basket on their backs and set off to pluck the tender tea leaves. They grew accustomed to what they had to do by asking other workers. Those first two or three weeks were pleasant enough. But they didn't care for the way the other coolie women spoke and behaved.

In the third week the old mother came down with malaria. She had to go to the hospital regularly after that, and take the medicines prescribed. Marudi would often go along with her to keep her company.

That was how the store manager of the estate saw her, at the hospital. Because she was a New piece of goods, she didn't understand what he meant when he said, "Have a bath and then come here." It was only after the business was concluded that she realized that this was the established custom among the coolies. For the old lady too, it was as if she had been hit in the stomach. It was only when they ventured to speak about it among their neighbours, they realized it was common practice. After that she wouldn't go anywhere near the store manager's place. But was it likely he would let go of her lightly? It was, after all, a way of life he could not change now. There was no other way but to give in to him. Marudi thought of her Vellayyan and shed tears. If only Vellayyan had been there!

The days went by. Marudi's baby was born. When she realized it was a girl, Marudi felt unbelievably sad. When she grew up, the child would experience the same fate as herself.

Because the old lady was there, it was possible for the child to be cared for. In that place, rife with malaria, what good was it, to possess every worldly comfort? What you needed was the will to live throbbing through your very pulse beat. And the baby, fortunately, possessed that.

When the tea blossom appeared, it meant that the Goddess of Malaria was hungry. Water dried up, even in the waterfall. That was the season when there was plenty of work. The coolies died in as large numbers as the mosquitoes born every day. If the tigers in that area killed and ate the coolies who had lived there for many years, even they got the fever. How could the old lady's frail body withstand so strong a disease? She went her way, forsaking Marudi and the baby. With the old lady's death, Marudi lost her mainstay and support, the loneliness of her life became fearful. But then, what does it matter how fearful the path is, if there is no other way?

God's compassion, though, didn't betray her utterly. If it took away her eyesight, it gave her a staff to lean on. The store manager was an individual who belonged to Kannappa Nayanaar's lineage. He offered to his deity, only the food which he himself had tasted and tried. He brought Mr Patrickson Smith along, one day, as if by accident. Smith's taste in women wasn't that bad either.

Marudi took her baby and went to live next to the bungalow, as the gardener to the durai.

And so, two years went by.

Sir Redmond Crown, the man who brought the family into prominence three generations before Sir Joseph Fitzmartin Crown, possessed that sterling British character which is the

---

Kannappa Nayanar, another Saiva saint, was a hunter called Tinnan. Out of his love for Siva, he offered worship in the best way he knew. He brought him flowers tucked in his own hair, water which he carried in his mouth, and the best meat from the hunt. After five days of this, Tinnan came to the shrine to find Siva's eyes bleeding. He gouged out his own eyes to engraft them on to the image. Siva then blessed him, restored his vision, and named him Kannappan, he who gave his eyes.

Pudumaippittan

very foundation of the British Empire. He had pestered his father, then a lowly clerk at some nameless bank, had set sail for Sri Lanka with the reputation of being the family vagabond, nevertheless had won money and fame on the tea plantations, and then married into a noble family.

Sir Joseph's only daughter, Maud Crown, had inherited the family ideals of three generations, their best attributes and their adventurousness. Her beauty, after the English fashion, was the kind to charm people and to hold them spellbound. Among her Set she was well known for her wild escapades. Suddenly she acquired a whim to go around the world by aeroplane. And then? Within ten days, the plane had to stop in Sri Lanka because of some fault.

A telegram flew to Mr Patrickson Smith. He arrived at Colombo, posthaste, bringing his motorcar. The two days following were spent in great merriment in Colombo. He realized that Miss Maud Crown was one who really knew how to enjoy life.

Maud Crown, who was also a great one for new experiences, liked everything she saw. Then they set off for the tea plantation, together.

In the bungalow, she had a room to herself. Marudi became her personal maid. Now, Miss Maud Crown was nobody's fool. She knew perfectly well how single men conducted themselves with black girls, on tea estates. All the same, she enjoyed being with a rake.

It seems to be a western belief that Cupid holds his court in warmer regions. So it should be no surprise that Mr Smith and Miss Crown became lovers.

Then ...

Vellayyan, released from prison, didn't return to the village immediately. Instead, he went straight away to his father-in-law's house. It was a great disappointment to him that he couldn't find Marudi there. His heart had been broken even before he left the prison. The thought of Marudi had been his only solace.

He borrowed some money from his father-in-law and set off for the tea plantation in search of Marudi.

He went on his way, imagining, as his father-in-law did, of Marudi in an ideal tea estate.

The single bus serving Vaaterpaalam arrived there in the evening.

As soon as he climbed down from the bus, he asked people standing there, about her. They pointed to the hut by the bungalow, sniggering a little.

He walked straight ahead, and saw in front of him, in the fading light, a couple, a durai and duraisaani, walking along, laughing and chatting, their arms about each others' waists.

Memories of Marudi filled his mind.

He arrived at the hut and knocked at the door. A weak voice came to him from within, "Who is it?" A crushed and heart broken voice. Vellayyan could not recognize it.

He pushed the door open, saying, "Is it Marudi?" Marudi was lying on a black blanket. Beside her the child lay, fast asleep.

A metal lamp smoked in a small niche above.

Vellayyan was shocked. Marudi was terrified, she thought she was seeing a pei. But then she thought, even if it was a ghost, it was her husband's ghost, after all. She sat up and asked, "Is it Vellayyan?"

It was, truly, Vellayyan. He stepped forward, to take her by the hand. "Don't touch me! Can't you see what's all over me?"

She showed him her arms and her back. She was covered in syphilis, the white man's disease.

Vellayyan felt as if he had been struck across the chest with a sledge hammer.

"This is how it is here."

Vellayyan made no reply to that. He said, "We must leave this place immediately."

"I can't make it. Take the child with you."

First, a flood of love for this child of his. Following that, bitter jealousy that she was not his.

"She is your own," Marudi told him.

"Swear it by your eyes?"

"I swear by my eyes."

A little later. "The old lady died only last year." Vellayyan didn't answer.

Marudi reached up and took out a metal box tucked under the roof. There were two hundred rupees in all, made up of five rupee notes. It was what the durai had given her, now and then.

"Savings from my wages. Take care of the child." She handed the notes to him.

Neither of them slept that night. When they had finished talking, it was dawn.

"Here," she handed the child to him. "Her name is Vellacchi."

A figure stood on the rocks, watching, until Vellayyan's head finally disappeared.

It stood there, looking towards the distant horizon, saying to itself, "Our village lies just there."

A smile. A great sigh.

The pannaiyar sat in the savukkai of Vasavanpatti, chatting about court matters. The evening had darkened. You could scarcely make out the man standing right in front.

A figure approached and stood at the verge of the path.

"Who is it?"

"Saami, it is Vellayyan."

"When did you turn up, lé? Now behave sensibly hereafter, mudhi! What have you got there in your arms?"

"My child, saami."

"That woman, Marudi, where's she?"

"She died, saami. Saami ... ?"

"What is it, lé?"

"The cash."

"Get along with you, you fool, you idiot. Keep it yourself. Try and use some commonsense hereafter."

"Commonsense!"

Several things happened in Vaaterpaalam following Vellayyan's visit. Even that slender attachment that Marudi had felt towards the world seemed to leave her, and disappear a long, long way. She thought of Vellacchi, all the time. She had been right to name the child Vellacchi. In this matter, and in bringing the baby and Vellayyan together, fate had been, for once, just.

The present that the durai gave her, before he returned to England with his new English girlfriend was syphilis. Its power over her gained ascendancy rapidly.

When the next durai arrived – and he was fanatic about hygiene – Marudi lost her position as gardener, and returned to being a tea plantation coolie. But nowadays the great gods didn't even deign to look at her. Instead of that, she considered herself lucky if she didn't receive abusive words.

In fact it was now the case that several of the neighbouring coolies brought her toddy, expecting favours in return.

Sometimes Marudi wondered whether she should just return to her village. If she were to do that, she would have to stay at her father's house. However much she longed to go to Vellayyan, she could not make up her mind to do that.

Within a short while of her arrival in the plantation, her figure and her youthful radiance had all changed. She was no longer the old Marudi, her lively chatter and her frequent laughter had all become past history.

Again and again she saw the same single scene happening in front of her eyes, Vellayyan carrying the child away, at dawn. The child, the child, the child. Always she thought of her. What would Vellacchi be doing now? Would she have learnt to speak yet? She dreamed of her all the time.

How could her frail body withstand the corrosion of memories and thoughts eating away into her all the time? She yearned to go to Vasavanpatti and die there, if die she must.

Nowadays, Marudi's arms and legs were covered in sores. She picked up whooping cough on top of that. The medicines prescribed by the hospital brought no relief, though she took them for many days. The doctor said she needed injections. That happened a few times, by the agent Subban's grace. What's more, her neighbour, Pecchi stayed with her and was able to help her.

Whatever happened, she was not allowed to stop from going out in the morning to pick the tea leaves. In this, kangaani

Subban was extremely strict. His usual punishments took the form of kicks, blows and verbal abuse. More cruel than that were the fines he levied, which ate away one's weekly wages.

One morning, by the time she was back from the hospital, it was getting somewhat late when she set off to pluck the tea leaves. She slung her basket on her shoulder. Anxious to avoid the area where kangaani Subban usually made his rounds, she hastened to the western side of the plantation, and began plucking leaves in a great hurry. The tea bushes next to her had grown tall and dense. She didn't notice that her friend and helper, Pecchi, and kangaani Subban were together on the other side. In that plantation, such a situation, was a common occurrence.

Subban, though, had seen her standing there. He imagined that she was staring at him. He was afraid she would make trouble for him, that some story might reach the durai's ears. It is common for all living creatures to spring upon their enemies in self-defence. And Subban was, after all, a living creature too.

Subban leapt on her and began to kick her, shouting abuse all the time.

Marudi stood stock-still, shocked out of her wits, wondering whether she was being attacked by a pei.

Subban grabbed her basket from her, emptied the leaves on her head, stamped on her chest. When he saw that the basket contained not leaf buds but fully developed leaves, he felt that his hand was greatly strengthened. Having beaten her up with the staff in his hand, he walked off in the direction of the offices, to record a fine levied against her.

Although Pecchi had wanted to intervene, she was terrified of Subban. Besides, she didn't have the heart to spoil it all when he was being quite nice to her. As soon as he disappeared, she

Pudumaippittan

came out from behind the bushes where she was hiding, and hastened to Marudi.

Marudi could neither breathe nor speak. Pecchi got some water from the nearby stream, sprinkled it on her and brought her back to consciousness. As soon as she came to herself, she was overcome by a fit of coughing. She spat up two or three drops of blood.

Marudi had to be supported physically and brought home to her hut.

After that incident, Marudi had no strength left in her, even to get up or walk about. At times, when the fever was raging, she would lose her conscious mind and laugh and talk as if she were playing with the child. It was only at such moments that the radiance which shone on her face in the early days of marriage, reappeared fleetingly.

When her mind cleared again, her eyes grew dim and the yearning of her broken heart was revealed in her features.

Pecchi had an idea. "You must write to her village," she told Subban. So a card was sent to Vellayyan. "Treat this as a telegram and come immediately."

Four days went by, and the new durai decided to cut down on the numbers of coolies on the estate. What is more, his plan was, in the first instance, to pay off the ones who were ill, and send them away.

Marudi's name went on the list.

As soon as this news reached Marudi, her brain cleared. Perhaps it was the sudden hope that she could go back to Vasavanpatti somehow, that gave her the strength to get about a little. But the weakness didn't leave her totally.

That very Wednesday, her wages and a ticket entitling her to a seat on the ship arrived.

By midday that Friday, the sun's dictatorship made Hitler seem a kind man. Marudi dragged herself like a cripple, along the path by the pond, towards the cheri. Given the state she was in, nobody would have recognized her. She had a stick in her hand, and there were bundles on her head and hip. In the bundle on her hip there were four or five kadali bananas and a pair of bangles – all for Vellacchi.

The sound of parai and thambattam drums came towards her from the cheri, quickening her footsteps. Once she turned the corner, there would be the village common. A little further on, Vellayyan's hut. She was almost at the Sudalaimaadan shrine.

Just then, in the midday heat, a procession came along, with drums and fanfare. Silamabam performers came ahead, accompanied by drumbeats. Behind them, in a chariot drawn by a single horse, a bride and bridegroom, in their wedding procession.

Marudi drew nearer to have a look. Her eyes dazzled. The bridegroom, adorned with flowers in his hair and sandalwood paste on his chest, wearing a gold embroidered cap, was none other than Vellayyan. How grandly he sat there! Marudi felt a burden drop away from her heart. Nobody had recognized her.

Suddenly she was seized by a fit of coughing. She spat on the ground. There were a couple of drops of blood there.

"Ei, mudhi! What does a bundle of grass cost?"

"Six annas, saami, take it or leave it."

"Give me a proper price."

"Of course it's a proper price. Six annas. Where do you want me to carry it?"

The man standing there was a liveried servant, wearing a red band and a brass badge, the servant of the Palayamkottai sub registrar. Opposite him stood Marudi. She was trying to gain the happiness she had hoped for in Vasavanpatti, here in Palayamkottai instead. Nobody in Vasavanpatti realized that Marudi had been and gone. There was a hospital in Palayamkottai. She could buy her medicines there. She had the courage and hope that there would be enough coolie work for her to make a living.

During the day, she cut grass and sold it. The money was enough for her daily needs. Perhaps there was something special about the Tamaraparani river waters. Anyway the worst of the illness and the sores which had erupted all over subsided. Although she was covered all over with the dark scars and sheen left by her disease, she wasn't all that badly off.

She agreed to bring the grass on a regular basis to the sub registrar's house. Because it would be a regular job, and she was to be given the money in hand every day, she accepted four annas a bundle.

Marudi's needs didn't increase. So she could actually save something even from so paltry a sum.

But her yearning to go and see her child grew more and more, every day. How was she to manage a visit? And that too, without Vellayyan's knowledge?

The child, the child. This was her constant thought.

When the registrar was required at a neighbouring town, she had a break of two or three days from the job of cutting grass. She could go to Vasavanpatti during that time, couldn't she?

She set off, taking a pair of glass bangles she had brought for Vellacchi from Colombo.

Until she actually started out, the problem of how she would meet Vellacchi hadn't struck her. Now she asked herself the question all along the way. How would she meet Vellacchi?

As soon as she had left the town behind her, Marudi held her bundle tightly against her waist and hurried as fast as she could. Visions came to mind, each minute, of how tall Vellacchi would be, what she would say to her.

It might have been about eleven in the morning when Marudi arrived at Vasavanpatti. She decided to take a circuitous route, where she was certain nobody would be about. By chance, not a single person she knew came towards her.

She had arrived at Vellayyan's hut. There were few people of her community in the streets. Were they zamindars, after all, that they could afford to sit at home all day? Didn't they have stomachs to care for?

Outside, opposite the hut, a dog barked.

Suddenly, from the hut, a small child's screams, the thud of blows falling, one after another. Following that, a woman's fury, in words. "You mudhi, you've overturned the pot of kanji. What will you eat now? When your father comes home, is he going to eat mud? Why didn't you get lost with that whore, your mother? ... You trash, you trash!"

Marudi's blood boiled. She charged inside the hut. She swept up the child that was being beaten, into her arms, and aimed a resounding blow at the cheek of the woman beating her.

If a stranger enters your house and beats you up, are you likely to keep quiet about it?

The battle took off at a great pace. They rained blows on each other, turn by turn. Blood began to appear on Marudi's face and chest.

Hearing them shout and scuffle, the child raised a great wail. The cheri women gathered around.

Some of the women took Marudi's side, a few took Vellayyan's second wife's side. But so far no one had recognized Marudi. Marudi didn't declare her identity, either.

But for how long will people stand by and watch a stranger entering an unknown house and beating up the inhabitants? In the end, the cheri's abuse and blows fell on her. Marudi was driven out. That evening, the little child, Vellacchi, disappeared.

Wouldn't any child agree to come away with a stranger who buys her fried gram and nice things to eat, when she is constantly beaten and abused at home?

By the time Marudi returned to Palayamkottai, it was nine at night. She was afraid that were she to stay there, they might follow her and catch up with her.

She went straight to the railway station in the dark, and lay down. She would have to go away elsewhere, somewhere far away. Very far away from these people.

Who can say Marudi never had any luck?

She met kangaani Subban at the railway station. He looked very fine in his white veshti and silver waist chain.

"Ei, Marudi, where are you off to, di?" he asked.

And then? kangaani Subban said he was on his way to Vaaterpaalam. He invited her to go with him. And she was ready to agree.

"Who is this child?"

"She's mine."

"Why are you bringing the creature there?"

"Even if she dies, she dies at my side."

Fourteen years have passed.

Having come away with kangaani Subban, Marudi spent all this time in Vaaterpaalam. But her position was no longer that of a plantation coolie, she was known as Subban's wife. And why shouldn't the status of wife accrue to her, after she linked her life to his for fourteen years?

Marudi had grown more stout, and somewhat odd-looking. She had lost two front teeth. Her hair was banded in grey on all sides. The other coolies wondered what potion she had given Subban. The reason was this. Whatever divine games Subban got up to on the sly, if ever anyone spoke ill of Marudi, he made sure they lived to regret it.

As for Vellacchi, she was the light of Marudi's life, and its entire reason. Now, it is impossible to live in Vaaterpaalam for fourteen years and remain unblemished. Vellacchi could talk about all kinds of things in graphic detail. But all of that was merely in fun. There was never any silence surrounding her. In fact you could be certain that wherever there was noise and laughter, Vellacchi was at its centre. Vellacchi had now come of age. She looked as Marudi had done when she first came, newly married, to Vasavanpatti – the very same features, the very same look. Marudi's great wish was to get her married into a Good family. She protected her daughter against the usual Vaaterpaalam crowd, in her own words, "As one would guard a fine piece of salt-fish." Vellacchi didn't loiter about, unemployed. She earned a little money as a tea plantation coolie. Vellacchi's wages were certainly not likely to fill their home with wealth, yet if she were to put the money aside, without spending it ...

Subban now worked as the chief kangaani on the plantation. So his salary had been raised a little. Now there was a little money to spare with which he could share a drink with others, besides himself, Marudi and Vellacchi. Subban was also experienced enough at behaving towards his senior managers in appropriate ways.

Besides, Subban was friendly with the long serving store manager of the plantation. This man was now well over fifty years old. Because he had lived there for so long, he had picked up some of the illnesses prevalent in Vaaterpaalam. The company was due to give him a pension and to retire him within that year. So he really wanted to place a relative of his in his position before he left the plantation. He also had a secret wish. He wanted to give his only daughter in marriage to his sister's son, and to place this young man in his own job. By way of fulfilling this aim, he invited Damodaran to Vaaterpaalam.

Now, just at this time, an order was sent out from the owners of the company, that a primary school should be established in Vaaterpaalam. A certain Ramachandran wrote in answer to the company's advertisement. And in time, the company appointed him as teacher in the school at Vaaterpaalam.

In the same bus that brought Ramachandran to Vaaterpaalam, there also travelled Maragatham, the store manager's daughter, on her way home for the school holidays. Maragatham was a fine looking girl.

The so called school was a small hut within a grove of teak trees, standing opposite the store manager's house. Inside it there were a table, a chair and a blackboard. Behind that was Ramachandran's rope cot. In front there were wooden planks for the children to sit on. Surely that was sufficient for coolie children?

To the right of the table there were four or five chairs, meant for the children of the managerial staff.

The total number of children attending the school was no more than twenty.

The doctor's two little girls and three boys belonging to tea store clerks were to begin their formal learning here, from now on. Then there were fifteen coolie children, none of them more than six years old.

Ramachandran was crazy about the teaching profession. He was driven by his ideals. Otherwise why would he finish his BA, spurn the job that was offered to him on his father's recommendation, and come here?

Ramachandran was also a good looking man.

He never made a difference between the children. The coolie children sometimes made him angry with their foolishness. Yet, when it was evening time, the children never went home without having played awhile with Saar. The children loved to hear stories. And if Saar started on one, they were never aware of time passing.

Ramachandran wanted to grow some flowering plants and bushes in front of his school, to make it more cheerful looking. There were no lack of roses, at any rate, in that place, where they grew wild, and in abundance. It was at the store manager's place that there were plenty of saplings of the other plants that he needed. And that was how Ramachandran and Maragatham happened to meet.

Ramachandran was watering the flowerbeds in front of the school, one day. School was over, and all the little children had gone home. There was silence everywhere.

His thoughts kept on returning to one person. Maragatham. At the same time, he felt that it was wrong of him to become too friendly with her. Yet after the lively chatter of the children throughout the day, his only desire was to talk to Maragatham.

It was at this time that Vellacchi came by.

"Anything the matter?" he asked. He had noticed Vellacchi before, but had never spoken to her.

"I want to learn to read. That's why I came," said Vellacchi.

"You want to read? Come at school time then, tomorrow!"

"I don't want to come then, like a big idiot. I'd feel ashamed. Why can't I come at this time?"

"But won't people get the wrong idea ... If you are alone with me?"

"Who'll dare to say anything? I'd break their teeth for them," said Vellacchi. The eagerness of her expression made him want to laugh. Such courage! Such innocence! He decided he would teach her.

"Should we begin straight away?" asked Ramachandran. He didn't expect that she would sit down, ready to learn, immediately.

He taught her the vowels, in their series, first of all. Half an hour passed.

"How many days will it take for me to read as well as Maragathamma does?" asked Vellacchi.

"I see that you really are keen," laughed Ramachandran. Then, "That's enough for today. Come tomorrow," he said.

"Very well," she said and stood up.

And just then, Maragatham came in, smiling, and calling out, "Vaadyaar, saar!"

She stopped short when she saw the two of them together, and all by themselves.

Ramachandran smiled and said, "This is my new pupil. She wants to read as well as you can, she says."

At the tone of his voice, Maragatham's suspicion disappeared. "Vellacchi wants lots of things! She's a terrible girl," she said.

Vellacchi ran away, calling out, "I'm going to learn to read, just like you!"

"My athaan arrived today. Will you come home?"

"Why do you want me to come now? Besides, the food I've cooked will go to waste."

"Is that so? Well, if you like I'll cook you a meal tomorrow, myself. Come, let's go."

"It doesn't look good if I butt in when you have guests. I'm sure to meet them very soon, anyway. Look, I'll come tomorrow."

"Are you going to listen to me or not?"

"If you are going to be so stubborn ..."

"What then?"

"Look, let me suggest a compromise. It's getting dark now. So let me walk with you half the way."

"You are stubborn enough to insist that a rabbit has three legs."

"No, no, I'd say three and a half. After all, haven't I half-listened to what you have said?"

"You don't have to listen to me at all," said Maragatham, turning round and walking off swiftly.

Ramachandran ran after her calling her name, and stopped in front of her. Her eyes were full of tears.

Pudumaippittan

"Should you start crying for such a small thing? ... Very well, I'll come then," he said, and started to walk along with her.

When they had gone halfway, she said, "Do you know why Athaan is here?"

"No, why?"

"To marry me."

"Is that so? Congratulations."

After that, neither of them spoke a word.

Vellacchi's lessons proceeded with great enthusiasm. She could recite her vowels and consonants by heart. She knew how to write them with some difficulty.

Ramachandran had a real affection for her. There was a certain sweetness in talking to her. Her innocent mind would show through frequently, although her language was as crude as that of a hardened prostitute.

Once the lesson was over, she would tell him about the affairs of the coolies, interspersing them with her own comments. Her attitude was that if you did something without anyone knowing about it, then it didn't count as a sin. However hard Ramachandran tried to make her change this attitude, he wasn't successful. All the same, through her familiarity with him she learnt to conduct herself blamelessly.

Marudi didn't like her daughter to go so frequently to the teacher's house. But however much she spoke to Vellacchi about it, it was no use. At the very mention of the teacher's house, Vellacchi would be up in arms.

Marudi really wanted to get her daughter married to Chinnaan, the groom who attended to the horses at the durai's bungalow.

Kangaani Subban agreed to the match. The matter reached as far as initial discussions. It was clear that Chinnaan would like to marry Vellacchi.

That evening, she arrived somewhat late for her lesson.

Ramachandran called to her, the children's reading book ready to hand, "Come in, Vellacchi. Come and sit in this chair. How is it you are so late?"

Vellacchi didn't answer. She didn't seem to take in anything Ramchandran was saying. She kept on sighing now and then.

"What's the matter, Vellacchi, you're not enjoying your lesson today, I think. If you like, we can put it off till tomorrow. Why do you look so out of sorts? Has there been a quarrel at home?"

"They say I mustn't come here any more. They want me to marry Chinnaan, the groom."

"Well, that's good, isn't it? I told you right at the start that people would talk. Do as Marudi tells you."

"Mustn't I come here any more? I don't like that fellow, Chinnaan, so ..."

"Never mind all that. Just do as Marudi says."

"But I *will* come, so there! They have threatened to tell the manager ayya and stop me by force. Why should these idiots mind if I learn to read?"

Ramachandran didn't know how to explain it all to her. Her stubbornness was that of a child. It seemed to him it would be best to calm her down and send her home. Yet he didn't wish to drive her away.

A sudden idea came to him. A totally crazy idea. What if he should marry her himself? Her childlike nature, her obstinacy, yet the love, which apparently had developed deep within her, all these attracted him. But would the two of them be compatible, given the caste difference?

"Vellacchi! Will you marry me?"

Astonishment, love and joy played over Vellacchi's features, wave upon wave.

"But why need we marry? ..." she asked, looking intently at him. In that glance were mingled her love, but also her fear because of the barrier between them.

Ramachandran understood clearly how her mind was working. She was capable of staking everything for his sake.

"Vellacchi! I'm not playing games. I'm asking you truly. Marry me," he said.

She drew close to him saying, "Very well."

Although the store manager was well over fifty, his ardour and desires showed no signs of abating. Nowadays, though, his Divine sports took place in secret. And the henchman who made them possible was Chinnaan.

For some time now, the store manager had his eye on Vellacchi. Now, in spite of their current prosperity, Marudi and kangaani Subban were known to be rough types. Besides, Vellacchi's character was well-known throughout Vaaterpaalam. But when was lust known to disappear that easily? Meanwhile Chinnaan knew perfectly well what was going on. He for his part had his eye on the kangaani's job.

The tea plantation spread for two and a half miles beneath the waterfalls. People were not to be seen often, in those parts. Beyond the boundary of the tea estate were the unspoilt forest reserves. The river, flowing down from the waterfall, made its way through the forest, leaping through the rocks.

The young girls who usually hung about with Vellacchi were bribed with small coins, to bring her to those parts, on the quiet.

They were girls who were also friendly with Chinnaan. They took a certain pleasure in entrapping Vellacchi, who had thus far never been caught. Everything went according to plan. Chinnaan arrived there with the store manager. Meanwhile, the young girls asked Vellacchi to begin work on the tea leaf sprigs, and then slipped away quietly.

Why go into details? The horse attendant grabbed hold of her brutally, and tied her to a tree.

There would have been no one about to hear Vellacchi's screams. But just that day, by chance, Ramachandran came that way.

Even from a distance he could make out Vellacchi's plight. But at first he did not even imagine it was Vellacchi herself there.

When he drew nearer, he understood it all. In a fury, as if he had gone mad, he attacked the two men.

Now, Chinnaan was a hooligan. Was it likely he would stand there quietly and take a beating? He plucked the stick out of Ramachandran's hands and hit out at him, as hard as he could, until Ramachandran fell down, unconscious.

When consciousness returned, first of all he heard Vellacchi's screams. Slowly he rose to his feet and untied the knots that held her.

Vellacchi flung her arms about him and sobbed her heart out. From time to time she raved in a thunderous voice like a wrathful Kali. Although Ramachandran was suffering unendurable pain, somehow he had to pull himself together. Otherwise how would they reach home?

Both of them made straight for Marudi's hut. When Marudi heard their news, it was as if she had been struck by a thunderclap.

So it turned out that this Chinnaan whom she had chosen so carefully to be her son-in-law, was henchman to the very same wretch who had once ruined her, so long ago. Screaming loud enough to bring the heavens down, she ran to the store manager's house. He had just finished eating, and had come out to the front of the house. Maragatham and Damodaran were standing next to him.

Running right up to him, Marudi flung a stone at him, shouting at the same time, "You ruined me, you wretch, and now you've destroyed my daughter." The stone struck him in the temple and at once plucked away his life.

Damodaran hit Marudi as hard as he could. She fell down in a faint.

Maragatham fell on her father's body, screaming. Various servants came and carried the old man inside.

By this time, news of what had happened spread among all the coolies. Everyone picked up staves and rods and ran towards the durai's bungalow. They believed that Chinnaan was to be found there. The durai came downstairs with his gun, having just woken up from his nap. The crowd, clearly, was not going to be controlled all that easily.

He went in again, summoned the Colombo police by telephone, and then fired at the crowd at random. The crowd set fire to Chinnaan's house. But Chinnaan wasn't a madman. He had made good his escape.

The crowd of coolies then made its way towards the store manager's house.

As soon as he realized that the coolies had gathered to riot, Ramachandran became very frightened. He was afraid of what they might do to Maragatham and the other inmates of the store manager's house.

He spoke of his fears to Vellacchi. At first she didn't agree, but then, because he wished it, she went there with him. It was only when they arrived at the house that they realized the full extent of what had happened. Ramachandran immediately took Maragatham and Damodaran away to the durai's house.

Vellacchi stood guard over Marudi. It was just then that the crowd approached the house.

Vellacchi possessed a wild courage. She called out to them, "The old man is gone. Don't do anything more now."

There were many in the crowd who did not share Vellacchi's view. All the same, their first frenzy had died down. Gradually, one by one, everyone left and went home.

Marudi regained consciousness. But her mind would not clear.

Ramachandran gave the durai an account of all that had happened. The durai, though, was a man of experience. As soon as he understood that the fault lay with the managers, he understood that there was no way out except to make peace. He had no wish to see the company's name bandied about in the papers.

The next day at dawn a police regiment arrived.

It was because of the durai that matters were concluded satisfactorily. The durai covered up the murder with utmost subtlety. His one desire was to keep it from the press.

Marudi never recovered her sanity. She, Vellacchi and Ramachandran disappeared elsewhere.

Quiet reigned once more in Vaaterpaalam. It forgot itself in tea cultivation.

And Maragatham? She is not in Vaaterpaalam either.

It is said that Damodaran is a teacher somewhere near Nellore. When you see Maragatham beside him, it certainly looks as if they must have got married. That is what most people say, too.

the great cremation ground

when evening falls, the city
changes, as if it wants to prove that civilization is just a highway
on which you can move forward only by jostling others, and, by
being jostled yourself, in return. But if you find yourself at the
junction of four or five streets and tramlines, the nerve centres
of the city's body, the nuisance becomes intolerable. People
returning from their offices, exhausted, people dressed to kill,
out to enjoy the gaiety of the evening, people who cannot afford
to travel by car but who still delude themselves that they are
fashion plates – all these will push and shove each other, and go
their own way, united only in their wish to prove that everyone
is exactly the same. On that day too, people went about their
business in just such a way.

"Mahamasaanam" was first published in *Kalaimagal* in 1941.

Ever since the Transport Department established its one way traffic rules, it is possible to see, from the tops of high rise buildings, the swirl of civilization down below. It is just like watching from the top of a dam while flood waters swell and flow beneath, bursting their banks.

The place I want to tell you about, is exactly like that. I mean the Roundtana at Mount Road. Rows of women with their baskets of fruit, bananas and mangoes. Behind them are women from the low caste communities of Chennai, who have just sucked at mango stones, spat them out, and then wiped their hands on their clothes, the Kabuliwala who walks about, raising his stick in salute, the Muslim beggar, the cripple, the leper, and the young woman preparing herself for her night's work. She sits at the verge of the road calmly, combing her hair and decorating herself. Then there are all these ordinary fellows, on all four sides, with their, "What, saar, it's been a long time," and "There's the bus," and "Get in."

Hurry, hurry, hurry.

It was at such a time that he lay on the pavement, dying slowly, at his leisure.

A good place to die. A comforting shadow from the trees. A setting sun from whom the worst of the heat had gone. The rush of the crowds, bustling with animation. You might have called it a right royal revelry.

He was dying at that time. Dying slowly, and at his leisure.

People went past him, came

towards him. They did not know what was happening, and some did not wish to know.

He was an old Muslim beggar. His beard had turned quite grey. He was covered in dirt-stained rags, old age and starvation together had shrunk his arms and legs. His feet were calloused.

There was another beggar sitting next to him, by his head. He lifted the old man's head, tried and failed to give him a gulp of water from a tin vessel, succeeding only in moistening his lips. He placed both his hands beneath the old man's head and tried to lift him up. The old man who was stretched out on the ground, the dying man that is, took hold of the rubbish bin thoughtfully provided by the founders of charitable institutions, and tried to raise himself. His eyes had dimmed. His lips bloomed blue. In a short while his story would reach its conclusion. Yet he did not loosen his hold on the bin. There was a certain solace in that grip. A certain strength. It wasn't exactly that he was conscious of someone at his side, offering him water. There was water, he must drink, that was all that was in his mind. He had no wish to think further than that, nor the need, nor the strength.

Just at that time two people came by, hoping to board a tram. They waited there awhile. The tram didn't arrive. Of the two, one was the father, about thirty years old. The other was a little girl, of perhaps four or five. He did not appear to be a man who found it a struggle to provide for his family. The child was unremarkable, but the care that her mother had taken over her was apparent in her bright yet unshowy appearance.

The child and the father stood there, waiting for the tram. The little one held her father's forefinger as she stood by his side.

Pudumaippittan

The mangoes in the vendor's basket, on the pavement opposite, looked tempting.

"Kunju, you must wait right here. Appa will go across and bring you mangoes," he said.

"All right," said the child.

"And you must never step on the road, or try to cross over, you understand? If you do, there won't be any fruit for you."

He was a little apprehensive about what he was doing. The child ought not to be left on her own.

"I'll stay right here, Appa," she said, as if she were making a solemn pledge, encouraging him to go.

And seduced by the mangoes, he crossed over to the other side, leaving the little girl on her own.

The child grew more brave. It was apparent that she was used to being left alone. Her eyes, having followed her father closely in her first fear, now began to wander about. A red car caught her attention, and she stood awhile, gazing after it. Someone in a great rush – who knows in what world his mind was wandering – knocked into her, making her stagger. The child gave up the pleasure of gazing at the red car, and in order to avoid being buffeted about, came and stood by the wall on the further side of the pavement. She leaned against the wall and looked about her in all directions, her hand in her pocket.

Her eyes now fell on the dying man and that other man who was helping him to die, and slowly, hesitantly she went towards them, wanting to watch what was going on.

The child knew that when she refused to drink her milk, her mother held the tumbler to her lips and insisted that she drink it down, but when her father said "No," she left him alone. Grown ups had the right to say "No." Even her mother was frightened of her father – these were the child's inferences. Now she was amused by what she saw. She was surprised that a grown man was being fed from a tumbler.

The child went closer to the two derelicts, to watch the fun. She came and stood by the old man's head.

The younger beggar was trying once again to wet the old man's throat. His hands were not sufficiently practised, though. When he tried to pour the water into the old man's mouth, it either splashed down on his neck, or it hardly left the tumbler.

The old man lay dying, holding on to the metal bin.

The child brought her lips together as if she were about to drink, and said, "Gently, gently."

The man who was administering the water looked up. He said, "Amma, you shouldn't be standing here. You'd better go somewhere else, amma."

"Why?" asked the child.

"This man is dying," said the beggar.

"Which means ... ?"

"He's dying, amma. He's going to die." He demonstrated by letting his head drop forward in a sudden movement.

The child thought this was hugely funny. "Do it again," she said.

Afraid that the crowds might gather, the beggar covered his mouth and motioned her off with his hand.

Two dambadi coins lay next to the old man's head, by way of indicating they would be for his last rites. The child's eyes fell on them now.

"Why don't you buy him some fried gram," she said, pointing to the money lying on the ground.

She was certain that everyone would like what she liked.

Pudumaippittan

Looking about him nervously, in case one of the older people there accused him of wrongdoing, the young man asked the child, "Have you got any money on you?"

"Here, it's a new coin," she replied, handing it towards him.

With a quick dart forward he caught it. It was a newly minted dambadi. Like millionaires hoping to end poverty by a few distributions of free food, their annadaana samaajam, or like one hoping to flavour the entire ocean by dissolving a handful of asafoetida in it, the child gave her gift of charity, her own daanam.

With dimmed eyes, still holding on to the metal bin, the old man was dying. People kept rushing to and fro.

A one anna coin fell to the ground, jolted from the hand of an individual who was rushing past. Completely unaware, the man walked on and was lost in the crowd, he was in such a hurry. The young man fell upon it. Then he looked about him, fearful of having been seen.

"Go away, amma," he said to the child, again, hoping to persuade her.

"Won't," she said, standing firmly, her legs spread apart. She pulled a face at him.

"Bawa, I'm going to fetch some milk," the young man said, getting up and making for the Hotel on the opposite side of the road.

The old man didn't hear him. He lay dying, holding on to the metal bin.

Now the child could see him properly. She went and stood close to him to watch the fun. Now the younger bogeyman, wasn't there to drive her away.

The old man was not conscious of the little girl standing there.

He was holding on to the broken bin, himself a battered and broken creature. To the child, all this was new, his face, his beard, the way his mouth was open. A fly came and sat on his bluish lip, then a second. She thought it was funny, the way he opened his mouth and twisted his lips in an attempt to get rid of them. For some reason, she called to him softly, just as the young man had done, "Bawa." She was a little afraid, in her heart. What if the buchaandi should sit up?

The old man lying there, opened his eyes wide. A fly came and sat on the pupil of his eye.

Then she heard her father's voice, scolding her.

"What are you doing di, standing there? I've been looking for you all over the place." It was the righteous anger of one who had bargained and fought, forced the vendor to agree to his price, and bought two mangoes at last.

Running up to him, she explained, "No, Appa, I was only watching the Bawa-buchaandi."

A few people turned to look at them.

He lifted up the child. Holding on to her mango with some difficulty, she sniffed at it, and then rubbed her nose against it saying, "It smells lovely!"

Pudumaippittan

kaanchanai

i just couldn't sleep that night, for no apparent reason. My mind was neither troubled, nor was it overflowing with happiness to keep me awake thus. I am just like everyone else. Yet my job is not like that of anyone else. I write fiction. That is to say, I spin yarns, and make a living out of the journalistic establishments that are prepared to accept them. My lies are accepted. Or in other words, they are recognized by the majority of the world as God, Dharma, et cetera, in various names and forms. This is what is called Creation, living in the land of the imagination et cetera. In fact liars like me are called other Brahmas, Second Creators. And I am the youngest in this lineage of duplicate Brahmas. When I think of all this, I feel some pride, certainly. Is the handiwork of Brahma false, too,

"Kaanchanai" was first published in *Kalaimagal* in 1943.

like ours? Am I false? If such philosophic queries occur around twelve o'clock at night, who won't begin to doubt his digestive system? "Ada, chut!" I muttered impatiently, and sat up.

This house had been built in such a way that one could sit up in bed and switch on the electric lights just by reaching out an arm. I did so. The sudden light troubled my eyes. My wife was fast asleep in the adjacent bed. What was she dreaming about? A smile played hide and seek at the corner of her lips. She was perhaps exulting in her culinary skills which could drag a man into philosophical inquiry right in the middle of the night. Stirring in her sleep, she moaned slightly and turned over. She was three months pregnant. Why should I wake her and make her sit up with me just because I couldn't sleep?

I put out the light immediately. I always feel a profound sense of peace, sitting in the dark. Isn't it true that at such a time, you become one with the darkness, united with the night, invisible to others? You can then drive that wooden cart – your own mind – wherever you please. People usually describe imagination as a chariot that can reach the place you wish to go to, the very moment you choose. But in reality, it is a wooden cart that follows along the thoughts of generations of human beings, from the earliest times to the present day – a path so frequently trodden upon that it has been turned into a beaten track. There are only the grooves made by wheels constantly

Pudumaippittan

grinding into the dust, and between them, a raised ground, less frequently walked upon. Occasionally the wheels have stumbled off the rut and on to the raised ground, giving those inside the cart a sudden jolt, otherwise it is always a gentle path, without peril, the track of well bred bullocks.

Lost in the comfort of thoughts, it seemed that in the dark I had smeared rather too much lime on the betel leaf. My tongue felt the sharp sting. Normally I don't bother about such things. If you choose to chew betel leaves in the dark, if you let go of the harness leaving your mind to roam at will, then you should not mind such minor disasters. With due respect, I tossed the tobacco, ready in the palm of my hand, into my mouth.

Chi! What a foul smell! Stinking like a putrefying corpse! Feeling nauseous, and wondering whether the tobacco I was chewing had been tainted, I went to the window, spat it out, and rinsed my mouth before returning to sit on the bed.

I couldn't stand the stink. It was as if a body had rotted and the stench was somewhere near. I couldn't stand it, couldn't understand it. Was it coming from the window? But there wasn't even the faintest breeze blowing. I left my bed and walked again to the window. I hadn't moved two paces before the stench completely disappeared. How extraordinary! I returned to the bed. There it was, again that foul smell. Was some dead creature lying under the bed? I switched on the light. Under the bed, there was only a cloud of dust that made me sneeze. I stood up and slapped myself free of dust.

My sneeze woke up my wife. "What is it, aren't you asleep yet? What's the time?" she asked, yawning.

It was exactly one minute after twelve.

And wonder of wonders! The stench had changed into a kind

of scent. The smell of incense sticks – in fact low grade incense sticks, the kind lit by the side of corpses.

"Can you smell something here?" I asked her.

"No, nothing at all," she said. After sniffing a while, she said, "There's a faint smell of incense. Someone must have lit them somewhere. I'm sleepy. Put out the lights and lie down."

I switched off the light. Traces of the smell still lingered. Going to the window I peeped out. Only starlight.

The shutters of the windows and the front door of the house trembled and banged softly. For just a second. Then silence. An earthquake, perhaps? In the starlight, a fruit-bat spread its wide leathery wings, flew towards the groves opposite, and disappeared beyond.

Both the stench and the scent had disappeared without a trace. I came back and lay down.

Next day, when I woke up at last from my pre dawn sleep, it was already late morning. I picked up the newspaper that had been flung through the window, and came out to sit on a cane chair in the front veranda. After creaking its objection, the chair bore my weight.

My life's partner came out, stood beside me and started complaining, "First of all you stay awake all night and then sleep late into the morning, and now if you come and sit here like this, what is to happen to the coffee?"

I had an unshakeable belief in Democracy and World Peace, and I was worried that both were being jeopardized by "The Advance of the Allied Forces, undeterred by any Resistance."

"All thanks to your elaborate cooking," I said, in a feeble counter attack, rising to my feet.

"You have nothing better to do, what else can you think of except to find fault with me? Well, it's no worse than the stories you write!" With this parting shot, she went towards the kitchen.

Bound by household rules, I went and cleaned my teeth, and then, holding the tumbler of scalding coffee with a towel, scanned the columns of the newspaper.

Just then a beggar woman, and a young one at that, came along, singing an unknown song. She stopped at our doorstep, calling out, "Amma, thaayé."

I glanced up sharply, then deciding that it was impossible to battle with beggars, put up my newspaper and built a fence around myself.

My wife came out to the front corridor, scolding the woman. "Aren't you able bodied? Why can't you earn a living by working in a few houses?"

"If I am given work, wouldn't I do it? My belly burns, thaayé. So far, I haven't got even a handful of rice from this street. Give me a piece of cloth to cover myself, amma." She started employing a beggar's usual arsenal.

"I'll give you work, but will you stay on? I'll give you food to fill your belly, clothes to cover yourself, what do you say?"

"Will that not be enough, amma? These days who is ready to give even that?" Saying so, she stood there, smiling at my wife.

"Shall I let her stay on and try her out for a couple of days? You know how easily I tire these days," my wife asked me.

"Chi, are you crazy? You want to engage a donkey of a beggar, who comes from heaven knows where? Can't you find anyone else in this entire world?"

The beggar woman, who was standing outside, chuckled.

There was a fatal charm in that laughter. My wife kept gazing at her, without once turning her eyes away. It seemed as if her entire will had become one with that nameless creature.

"Can't you tell a person from her face? You come in, amma," countermanding my orders, my wife took her inside.

And the deceitful beggar followed her, rejoicing within. What! I rubbed my eyes and stared at her feet. They walked in the air, a minuscule distance – the height of a kunrimani seed – above the ground. I felt a shiver go through me. Was it an illusion? When I looked again, the beggar woman glanced at me with a smile. Ayyo, was that a smile! As if a spear of ice had struck through my bones to the marrow, it nearly killed me with terror.

I called my wife to my side. I told her that it wasn't good to have this woman in our home. But she, for her part, insisted most obstinately that she must have this stranger for her servant. Is there no end to the odd desires of early pregnancy? My heart beat fast in certain anticipation of disaster. I peeped at her feet again. They touched the ground like everyone else. What was this strange illusion?

Tenali Raman proved that it was impossible to turn a black dog into a white one. My wife, on the other hand, established that we can turn even beggars into the same kind of human beings we ourselves are. It was clear that once the beggar woman had bathed, washed her hair and put on clean, though old, clothes, she was fit to sit next to anyone and talk to them as an equal. It seemed that this woman was adept at amusing conversation. I heard frequent chuckles and giggles. I was surprised at the way she waited on my wife, hand and foot. My own fears of a while ago seemed to mock at me.

Pudumaippittan

It was dusk, the darkening hour. My wife and that maid were sitting together, laughing, telling stories. I had turned the lights on in the front room and was observing her under the pretext of reading a book. Between the hall where I sat, and the room where they were, there was a central area. I had hung a mirror there. Their reflections were clearly visible in it.

My wife told her, "You've roamed about everywhere, haven't you? Tell me a story."

"Yes, it's true I've been to all sorts of places like Kasi and Haridwar. I was told a story once, in Kasi. Shall I tell it to you?"

"Yes, tell me. Tell me the story."

"They say it was five hundred years ago. The Raja of Kasi had an only daughter. It was said that you could not find another to match her beauty. The Raja also wanted her to be learned in all fields. The guru chosen for her was a great sorcerer, he knew everything there was to know about magic, devices, strategies. And he had an eye on the princess. She, however, wanted to marry the prime minister's son.

"Somehow he found out about this. Who found out? That guru."

This was a miracle! Was I listening to the story she was telling my wife, or was I reading its account in the book I held in my hands? The book was an English one, called *Historical Documents*. The story of the King of Varanasi's daughter was staring at me, in print. The last line of the page that was open in front of me was an English translation of the words, "He found out about this." My head began to spin. I broke into a sweat. Was I going mad? I kept my eyes fixed on the open page. The print began to dim.

Suddenly, devilish laughter! With the sharpness of an explosion, it seized my entire mind. I looked up with shock. My gaze fell on the mirror. Reflected there, I could see a loathsome figure, its teeth bared, laughing in frenzied intoxication. I had seen many repulsive figures – those that appeared in my own dreams, and those imagined by the sculptor's chisel. But I had never seen anything as horrifying as this. The horror was apparent only in the teeth and the eyes. In the rest of her features there was a wonderful serenity, mesmerizing the onlooker. In the eyes, a blood thirstiness. In the teeth, a greed to tear at the flesh and gorge upon it. Behind this faint image, tongues of flame from the fire of the kitchen hearth. I gazed at it, lost to everything. In a minute the image disappeared. The next minute it was the beggar woman's face reflected there.

"I simply forgot to ask your name." My wife's question reached my ears.

"Why not call me Kaanchanai? Like the Kaanchanai in the story. It doesn't matter what you call me. It's just a name, after all."

My heart would not consent to leave my wife alone with her. Heaven knew what might happen. Once the mind is overtaken by fear, can there be a limit to the trembling within?

I went inside. They were merrily chatting.

When I entered, having summoned a forced smile, I was greeted with barbed words. "What business do you have amongst us womenfolk?"

The woman who called herself Kaanchanai was bent low, chopping something. A smile brimming with mischief played at the corner of her mouth. Unable to say anything further, I became the sentry once more, standing guard behind my book fence. My wife, after all, was pregnant. Could I frighten her? How, else could I protect her?

We ate and then went to bed. The two of us slept upstairs. The woman called Kaanchanai slept in the front room.

I was merely lying on the bed. Did not close my eyelids. How could I? Heaven knows how long I lay like that. My heart was beating fast, wondering whether last night's smell would return.

Somewhere a clock began its process of striking the midnight hour.

The echo of the eleventh stroke had not yet died away.

Somewhere a door creaked.

Suddenly, sharp nails fell upon my hand, scratched across and slid away.

Shaking all over, I sat up. Thank goodness, I did not babble.

It was my wife's hand that had fallen thus.

Was it really hers?

I got up, bent over and observed her closely. She was fast asleep and breathing steadily.

I was eager to go down and investigate, but afraid!

I went. I climbed down softly, my footsteps making no noise.

It felt as if a whole yuga passed by.

Quietly I peeped into the front room. The outside door was closed. Moonlight streaming in through the open window nearby, pointed to the empty mat and pillow.

My legs wouldn't hold up. They trembled violently.

Without turning around, walking backwards, I reached the stairs. Had she gone upstairs, perhaps?

I hurried upstairs.

It was quiet there.

As peaceful as before.

My mind would not clear.

I stood by the window and watched the moonlight.

There was no human movement to be seen.

Only a dog howled somewhere, raising a lament which faded away.

From the opposite corner of the sky a giant bat flew towards our house.

As I stood watching, my fear began to ebb. I became calm, assuring myself that it was an illusion.

But downstairs?

I was eager to see once more.

I went downstairs.

I didn't have the courage to go in.

But there! Kaanchanai was indeed sitting on her mat. She smiled at me. A poisonous smile. My heart froze. Pretending to be calm, I went up the stairs, muttering, "What is it, can't you sleep?"

Was there a smell of frankincense then? I seem to remember it being there.

When I woke up, it was very late.

My wife woke me up saying, "What's happening to you, as time goes on, you seem to be sleeping the days away. The coffee is getting cold."

At daytime, when darkness or fear do not have a place to hide, everything certainly looks different. But deep within the mind, fear had taken root. How was I to get rid of this danger?

Can you seek comfort by sharing with someone else the

Pudumaippittan

mental torment you experience because of your wife's adultery? This situation was like that. Suppose someone like me, someone who boasted that he was doing a literary service to society at large, and who fooled himself into believing it, were to go about saying, "Saar, a pei, a she-devil, has come to live in our house. I am terrified that she might harm my wife. Can you advise me how to get rid of this peril?" People would surely wonder whether I was making fun of them, or whether I had gone mad. To whom could I explain it all and ask for help? How long could I stand guard?

How was this all going to end? What disaster was there in store? I was in a quandary, neither able to speak about it nor to swallow it all quietly. Heaven knew what magic potion this new servant had given my wife. They spent their time together without the slightest burden on their hearts.

That day, morning and night seemed to chase each other. And I had never known time to pass by so quickly.

At night, as we were about to go to bed, my wife announced, "Kaanchanai is going to sleep upstairs, in the room next to ours." I felt as if a lighted fire had been placed in my lap.

What plot was afoot?

I will not sleep at all. I will spend all night sitting up, I decided.

"What is it, aren't you going to lie down?" asked my wife.

"I'm not sleepy," I answered. Terror, like a sharp spear, pierced me.

"As you wish," she said, lying down on her side. And that was it. She was fast asleep. Was it an ordinary sleep?

I too wearied of sitting up so long, lay down, thinking I'll rest my body.

It began to strike twelve.

What is this smell!

My wife, lying next to me, screamed in an inhuman voice. Among those meaningless sounds which gushed out in the guise of words, I could make out the single name, "Kaanchanai."

I switched on the light immediately and shook her, again and again, to awaken her.

She came to herself and sat up, shuddering. Rubbing her eyes, she said, "I felt as if something bit my throat and sucked my blood."

I peered at her throat closely.

At the hollow of her throat, there was a tiny spot of blood, like a pinhead. Her entire body was shaking.

"Don't be afraid," I lied deliberately. "You must have thought of something strange as you fell asleep."

Her body was trembling. She slid back on the bed in a faint.

At that very moment there was the sound of a temple gong.

Some strange song in a cacophonous voice.

A voice, calling out with authority, "Kaanchanai! Kaanchanai!"

A wild scream which seemed to shake my entire house. All the doors banged repeatedly.

Then a silence. The deep silence of the cremation ground.

I got up and peeped towards the entrance of the house.

A man stood in the middle of the street. What a countenance!

"Come here," he signalled. Like a puppet on a string, I climbed down the stairs and went out.

As I passed the room where Kaanchanai slept, I could not help looking inside. As expected, she wasn't there.

I went into the street.

He said, "Rub this on amma's forehead. Kaanchanai won't trouble you hereafter. Go and do it immediately. Don't wake her up."

The vibhuti felt hot.

I brought it inside and rubbed it on my wife's forehead. Was it ordinary vibhuti? I couldn't be sure. I certainly remembered he did not hold a bell in his hand.

Three days passed.

As she gave me my coffee in the morning, my wife said, "These men are all like that." What could I say?

deliverance from the curse

along the path, a stone statue. a
form so beautiful that it inspired a leaping desire in the most
weary onlooker. It was as if a sculptor of rare ability had appeared
on this earth for this single work alone, and had put all his
dreams into stone. But from the eyes of the figure, a sadness –
an inexpressible sadness – springs, overcoming the desires and
lust of her onlookers and plunging them into sadness, too. For
this is no sculptor's dream. This is the result of a curse. This
indeed is Ahalya.

She lies in the forest path, a tragedy in stone, on Nature's lap.
And Nature, like a renunciant, looks upon her tragedy with

"Sabavimochanam" was first published in *Kalamagal* in 1943.

Author's note: For those acquainted with the Ramayana, this story might be
incomprehensible, unpalatable too. I am not concerned about that.

impartial eyes. The sun beats down. Dew descends. The rain falls in abundance. Dust and chaff, sparrows and small owls sit on her, and fly away. She lies there unconscious, a tapasvi lost in her penance, a stone.

Some distance away there is an ant heap. Lost in meditation, empty of thoughts, forgetting his sorrow, Gotaman performs his austerities. Nature, impartial, protects him too.

Still further off, in the same way as the cage of the couple's family life collapsed without a crossbeam, so too the roof that gave them shelter has fallen down for lack of support, has become dust, has scattered with the wind. The walls have disintegrated. All that is left now is the raised ground. It looks like the scar of the sorrow which filled their hearts.

In the distance, the rustle and ripple of the Ganga. Mother Ganga. Is she aware of the infinite tragedy of these two?

And so, aeons have passed by.

One day ...

The early morning sun was harsh enough. Yet the greenness and shade from the creepers, together with the kindly breeze, brought a certain comfort to the heart – like a religion which attempts to hide the sorrows of this world, and to inspire belief and courage.

Viswamitra comes striding along, majestic, like a lion, reliving in his mind the sheer joy of having completed the duty he had taken up. Maaricha and Swaku are not to be seen anywhere. That ancient malevolence, Taadaka, has been crushed. He enjoys the satisfaction of having been the means of bringing tranquillity to all those engaged in dharmic concerns, meditation and sacrificial offerings.

He turns round frequently, looking behind him. Such a tenderness in that glance! Two young boys come along, playing, chasing each other. They are none other than Rama and Lakshmana, children descended from the gods. They have already begun the destruction of the rakshasas, but do not yet understand its import. They run along, chasing each other.

Their game of chase raises a cloud of dust. Lakshmana comes running ahead, Rama is chasing him. Viswamitra, himself full of joy, turns round to see what the boys' hilarity is about. He stands still and gazes.

The dust cloud falls and spreads on the statue.

Within the statue, the heart that stopped and turned to stone, heaven knows when, begins to throb once again. The blood that clotted and dried in its many tracks begins to flow. A life-warmth pervades the stone and it becomes living, rounded flesh. Awareness returns to it.

Ahalya shuts her eyes and opens them. Her consciousness awakens. Deliverance! Deliverance from the curse!

Oh God! This fleshly body, once tainted, has been purified.

And the divine being who gave her, once again, a new life? Could it be that child?

She falls at his feet, folds her hands and makes obeisance. Rama looks towards the rishi in surprise.

Viswamitra understands at once. She must be Ahalya, Gotaman's wife. That artless girl who was deceived by Indra in his magical disguise. Because of her excessive love for her husband, she allowed herself to be deceived by that magic disguise, allowed her body to be used. All this, Viswamitra tells Rama. You see that ant-heap there, there he is, lost in meditation, forgetful of himself, like the butterfly in silent penance in its cocoon. Look, he too stands up now.

His eyes, coming out of deep meditation, swirl around, like knives just sharpened on a whetstone. The life-force knits and courses through his body as if he has been fed on an elixir. He comes forward in haste, yet with some hesitancy, as if he cannot quite free himself from the woman's disgrace.

Once again, this snare of sorrow? His mind had not considered what sort of life there could be, after a deliverance from the curse. For the present, it still encircles his life, like a gigantic wall. She too is lost in perplexity.

Rama's entire education had trained him to look with the eyes of dharma. With the clear light of knowledge. He had not yet been sharpened against the whetstone of experience. Yet he had been taught by Vasishta, who could look steadily upon each separate braided thread in life's tangles without breaking it. There was no smallness about him. He had the courage as well as the wisdom to strike upon a new path.

What kind of world is this that ties itself into these troubling knots? Should someone be punished for something that happened without the assent of her conscious will and reasoning mind? "Amma," says Rama, falling at her feet.

Both rishis (the one who thought boldness essential to knowledge, and the other who saw that love alone is the basis of dharma) understood the youth's perspective and his reasoned conclusions, and they rejoiced. What an easy truth. Full of love yet so daring.

Viswamitra says, quietly, "It is only right that you accept her, she did not err in her heart."

In the cooling air, the different harmony in his voice is apparent.

Neither Gotaman, nor his wife, nor that scarred foundation without pillars, their former hut, had moved. Yet sentient life began to manifest itself in that once-dead place.

The forces that had come there to change the entire course of their lives, as if with a whiplash had now disappeared. Should they not try to reach Mithila at least by nightfall? Married life beckoned, with both hands.

Gotaman could not speak to her, as he could once, from an unblemished heart. It was as if his burning accusation of her as a harlot, that day, so long ago, had succeeded only in scorching his own tongue. What could he say? What should he say?

"What would you like?" asked Gotaman. In the swirl of emotions, commonsense and wit had deserted him and he could only push out these meaningless words.

"I am hungry," said Ahalya, like a child.

Gotaman went to a nearby field and gathered all kinds of fruit. The desire and love which had played over everything he did in the very first days of their married life was apparent once again, in the movement and stillness of his hands.

After all, our marriage only came to flower after we found pity and sympathy for each other, after an early disappointment. I only gained her hand after circling the divine Kamadenu. So said Gotaman's heart, changing direction, accusing himself.

Ahalya ate her fill.

Between them flowed absolute compassion.

Yet each was in anguish, trapped in a different prison.

Pudumaippittan

Ahalya's only concern was whether she was right for Gotaman. Gotaman's only concern was whether he was right for Ahalya.

The flowers that bloomed along the forest path watched them and laughed.

Deferring to Ahalya's only wish, Gotaman built a hut some distance away from the outer walls of Ayodhya, by the shores of the Sarayu, where the stench of humankind would not reach them. And there he studied the meaning of dharma. Now he had absolute faith in Ahalya. He would not have doubted her, even if she were to lie on Indra's lap. He believed her to be infinitely pure. And he was now in such a position that without her daily help all his philosophic enquiries would have been just dust and chaff.

Ahalya nourished him with her immeasurable love. At the thought of him, her mind and body felt overcome with the tenderness of a newly wedded bride. All the same, the stone that had entered her heart had not quite moved away. She wanted to conduct herself always in such a way that no one would have reason to doubt her, not even to look at her in a particular way. Because of this, she forgot how to be natural. Her behaviour had changed in character. Everyone around her appeared to her as Indras. Fear entered her heart and froze it. The easy chatter and play of her former days deserted her, totally. Before she uttered anything, she repeated it like a lesson, a thousand times in her mind, examined each word, from all perspectives, to make sure it was the right one. She agonized over even casual words that Gotaman spoke, wondering whether they contained some other meaning.

The very business of living became a hellish torment.

The other day, Marichi, the great rishi, had visited them. Some while ago Dadichi had come to their home. Matanga had looked in, on his way to Varanasi, enquiring after Gotaman's health. Although they were all full of concern and goodwill, Ahalya shrank from them. Her mind closed in on itself. She could scarcely bring herself to give them the hospitalities due to guests. She was too shy to allow her clear eyes to meet even an ordinary gaze from other people. In the end, she hid herself in the hut.

Nowadays, Gotaman's thoughts turned towards a different kind of enquiry. Now he held that all the fences and strictures of dharma applied only to those who acted in full consciousness of what they were doing. If a violation of the moral law happened without one's awareness and assent, then even though the entire seed of man is crushed because of it, yet it could not be judged a sin. The full intention of the mind, and the deed we do with such intention, is what marks us. Living in a broken down hut, and starting once more from a position which was only the collection of other peoples' ideas, Gotaman turned his thoughts in a new and different direction. In his mind, Ahalya walked about, sinless. It was he who had been unfit to accuse her, the anger which had invoked his fiery curse had tainted him alone.

From time to time, Rama and Sita would come in their direction, by chariot, on a pleasure trip. The god-child, in Gotaman's imagination, had grown into the ideal youth. His laughter and play were like ever-burning lamps, and sufficient commentary to the Dharmasastras. That rare affinity between those two young people! It reminded Gotaman of his own life of long ago.

Sita was the dove who came to ease the burden upon Ahalya's heart. Sita's very words and smiles seemed to wash away

Ahalya's stains. It was only when she visited that Ahalya's lips would part in a smile. Her eyes would betray a dawning light of happiness.

Growing up under the surveillance of Vasishta, were they not destined to be the ideals of rulership? The young couple came to the rishi and his wife who lived in seclusion on the banks of the Sarayu, each in a separate world. They revived a former liveliness within them.

Ahalya had no wish to go out and engage with the world about her. Sita's nearness alone eased her heart's burden and gave her a little courage.

She agreed to come to Ayodhya for the grand occasion of the pattabhishekam. But how fierce the emotional whirlpool in the palace turned out to be! In one breath, Dasaratha's life was taken, Rama driven into the forest, Bharatha distressed, in tears, forced to go and live in Nandigramam.

Some great force, impossible to measure in human terms, made it all happen, like a dice rolling in a headlong frenzy which brings the game to an end once and for all.

With what scrupulousness Vasishta had watched over his wards, wishing to establish an ideal governance, the triumph of humankind's dharma! All his calculations had become mere dust and chaff, dwindled to the glimmering light standing alone in Nandigramam.

It has to be said that the little hut by the Sarayu collapsed once again for lack of support. Gotaman's philosophic investigations were scattered by the whirlwind. Belief dried up in his mind, leaving it waste and void.

And Ahalya? Her sorrow cannot be measured nor told in words. She could not understand it, she was totally crushed.

Rama went away to the forest. His younger brother followed him. Sita too. Her heart was as heavy and dark as it once had been when she was a stone statue. Being alive, though, the consciousness of its weight was unbearable.

At earliest dawn, Gotaman finished his prayers and austerities, came ashore, entered his hut.

Ahalya was waiting with the chembu of water to wash his feet. Her lips moved.

"I cannot bear to be here any more. Why don't we return to Mithila?"

"Why not. Let's go. It's a long time too since we saw Sadanandan." And he made ready to leave.

They began to walk towards Mithila. A heaviness had entered each of them and inhabited their hearts.

Gotaman stopped. He reached out and took Ahalya's hand as she came up towards him, and walked on. "Don't be afraid," he said.

They walked on towards Mithila.

Dawn broke. They walked along the banks of the Ganga.

Someone stood in the water, reciting the Gayatri in a bell-like voice.

The couple waited on the shore, some distance away, until the prayer was said.

"Sadananda!" called Gotaman.

"Appa ... Amma." Sadanandan poured out his happiness, and fell at their feet in greeting.

Ahalya embraced him in her heart. How much like a stranger her child Sadanandan had become, moustached and bearded like a rishi!

The radiance of his son's face brought ease to Gotaman's heart.

Sadanandan invited both of them to his hut. He made every arrangement for their comfort and then prepared to set off for Janaka's court and forum of discussion.

Gotaman readied himself to go with his son. Of course the son wanted his father to accompany him. Yet, he thought for a moment with special filial compassion, of the long journey that the older man had just undertaken. But then again, Gotaman's body had withstood the rigorous austerities of aeons, how could a short walk tire him out? Sadanandan followed Gotaman. He was eager to learn about his father's new philosophic enquiries.

As he walked along the streets of Mithila, it seemed to Gotaman that a certain weariness of spirit and of sorrow, growing out of Ayodhya, had pervaded this city, too. It was as if a suppressed sigh had mingled with the very wind.

People went to and fro, they went about their business, everything was done as if in selfless service. There was no involvement, no intense participation.

There was no enthusiasm in the elephant's stride as it carried the sacred waters for the ritual bath of the deity, nor the play of grace on the features of the accompanying priest.

They entered the debating forum. An army of disputants filled the chamber, like an ocean. How could any real discussion even enter such a marketplace, Gotaman wondered. In the end, he found he had been mistaken.

Janaka's eyes fell on them immediately.

He came hurrying up towards them, offered the sage argya, greeted him with all due observances, and invited him to sit next to himself.

Janaka's face was touched with sadness. Yet there was no hesitancy in his speech. It was clear his mind had not lost its tranquillity.

Gotaman hesitated, wondering what he should say.

Stroking his beard, Janaka spoke. "When he established the state, Vasishta did not build in a sluice-gate for emotion."

Janaka's words touched a nerve centre.

"Isn't it from that whirlpool of emotion, that truth is born?" asked Gotaman.

"Sorrow too, if we have not learnt to use our emotions. When we wish to establish a state, we must take account of this, or there can be no state," Janaka said.

Gotaman voiced a doubt, "What of yours, though?"

"I don't reign, I try to understand rulership," said Janaka.

Both were silent awhile.

"What is your enquiry into dharma about?" Janaka asked, courteously.

"I have not even started on it yet. I can only try and understand from now on, so many puzzles and mysteries ensnare my senses." Gotaman arose as he said this.

From the next day, he stopped attending Janaka's forum. His mind was full of enigmas, standing as high as the Himalayas. He needed solitude. Yet he didn't seek it. Ahalya should not be hurt, after all.

The very next day, Janaka asked, "Where is the great muni?"

"He spends his entire time beneath the asoka tree in front of our hut," replied Sadanandan.

"In austerities?"

"No, just in thought."

"The storm has not abated," said Janaka softly, to himself.

Ahalya took immense pleasure in bathing in the river. Here, certain of peace and quiet along the Ganga, she would set off at earliest dawn with her water pot.

For a couple of days, alone in the river, she could allow her thoughts to branch out as they wished, unburdening herself, she could play in the river, bathe, and return at last with a full water pot.

It did not last.

She was walking home after her bath, eyes cast down, letting her thoughts drift.

She could hear the sound of toe rings coming towards her. Rishis wives whom she did not know, they too were on their way to bathe. But as soon as they saw her, they started as if they had seen an outcaste, and then turned and fled, shunning her.

From a distance she heard their voices, "That was Ahalya." Those words burnt into her more painfully than the fiery curse which came flaming out of Gotaman's belly.

In an instant she felt as if her inner self was on fire, like a cremation ground. She was distraught. "Oh God," she sobbed, "Even though I am absolved of the curse, am I not to be absolved of the sin?"

She served Gotaman and Sadanandan their food like a mechanical doll. Her mind was beating out a refrain, "My son has become a stranger; strangers have become enemies, why stay here any longer?" Like one returning to reality from time to time, Gotaman placed a mouthful of food in his mouth, and then became lost in thought.

The heavy atmosphere wrought by his parents' bewilderment made Sadanandan too gasp for breath.

In order to lighten the air, he said, "The sage Atri was here, to visit Janaka. He has been to visit Agastya. He's travelling towards Meru now. Rama and Sita paid their respects to Agastya, it seems. Apparently Agastya told them, It's a good place, Panchavati. Stay there awhile. It looks as if they have done just that."

Ahalya asked softly, "What if we too should make a pilgrimage?"

"Shall we start now?" asked Gotaman, standing up and washing his hand.

"What? Immediately?" asked Sadanandan.

"It doesn't matter when," answered Gotaman, collecting his staff and kamandalam, and setting off towards the front door.

Ahalya followed him.

Sadanandan's heart was heavy.

The day was dying, the light had dimmed. Two people were walking along the shores of the Sarayu, towards Ayodhya.

Fourteen years had gone by, vanished, mingled now into the flood of time. There was no eminent sage they had not met, no sacred place of pilgrimage they had not visited. Yet they had not gained peace of mind.

They stood on snowy mountain crests and looked with adoration upon Kailasa rearing in front of them, beyond the reach of those who do not possess courageous feet, like Sankara's imagined temple, beyond the reach of timid minds.

They crossed a desert which was identical to their inner drought, their burden of sorrow, their lack of belief.

They circumambulated volcanoes, which, like their own minds spouted flames and threw up the dregs of smoke, ashes and dust.

They reached seashores where the waves tossed endlessly like their hearts. They returned.

They crossed hills and valleys, like the crests and troughs of their own lives.

A single hope had dragged them onwards, "In a few days

more, Rama will return. After this at least we may see a renewal of life."

They arrived at the place where fourteen years ago they had left the cottage they once built, desolated.

That very night Gotaman repaired it, so that it was a fit dwelling once more. When the work was done, the rising sun was smiling.

They bathed in the Sarayu and returned.

Ahalya busied herself in serving her husband. Both of them longed for and looked forward to the day of Rama's and Sita's return. All the same, how can we cross the rules of established time, except through the imagination?

One day, Ahalya set off early in the morning to bathe in the river. Before her, someone else, a widow, had finished her bath, and was returning. Although she could not tell who it was, the other woman had recognized her. She came running forward and fell at Ahalya's feet, her entire body prostrate on the ground.

Devi Kaikeyi, without her retinue of attendants and maid servants, alone, a renunciant?

Ahalya set down her water pot and lifted her up with both hands. She could not understand Kaikeyi's gesture.

"Bharatha is so engrossed in dharma that he has forgotten to give me a place in his heart," said Kaikeyi.

No anger throbbed in her voice, no leaping arrogance. The Kaikeyi she had imagined and the Kaikeyi in front of her were different people. All Ahalya saw was a yearning heart, like a vine without a supporting frame.

They walked on towards the Sarayu, their arms still about each other.

"And who was the cause of Bharatha's steadfastness in dharma?" asked Ahalya. A gentle smile of compassion touched the edge of her lips, and then disappeared.

"If a fire started by a small child razes the city, should we kill the child?" asked Kaikeyi.

Ahalya thought it was certainly necessary to raise a fence between the child and the fire. "But what was burnt was indeed burnt and lost, wasn't it?" she asked.

"Then is it enough just to heap up the ashes and sit by them without cleansing the entire city?" asked Kaikeyi again.

"The person who will remove the ashes will arrive in a couple of days, though," Ahalya reminded her.

"Yes," said Kaikeyi. There was a profound contentment in her voice. It was not Bharatha who looked forward the most to Rama's return, but Kaikeyi.

The next day when she met Ahalya, she looked as desolate as if her whole inner self had collapsed.

"Our messengers have been sent out in all directions. There is no sign whatever, of Rama. How can we hope that they will be here within the next forty naazhigai? Bharatha has declared he will perform the praayopavesam and give up his life. He is already arranging for the sacred fire to be lit," Kaikeyi told her.

She implied that Bharatha wished to extinguish his life at the fire, as an atonement for the love of rulership that had been forced upon him.

After a pause, Kaikeyi went on, "I too will enter the fire, but alone and in secret." Her inner resolve shone.

After fourteen years, once again the very same whirlpool of

Praayopavesam: An old Vedic rite, literally "waiting for death," whereby a man abstained from food and drink, and sat on sacred darbha grass, preparing to die.

emotion. Had the results of that curse that fell upon Ayodhya still not ended?

Ahalya's thoughts flew about, without connection. She even wondered whether that curse had not come from the shadow of her own feet.

"Can you not ask Vasishta to stop him?" she asked.

"Bharatha will be bound only by dharma and not by Vasishta," said Kaikeyi.

Ahalya was outraged. "A dharma that is not bound by human beings is the enemy of the human race."

A foolish hope that Bharatha might, perhaps, submit to her husband's advice, struck her. She was terrified that the wheel of tragedy would begin to turn once more in Ayodhya.

Gotaman agreed. But his words were profitless.

But, after all, Agni did not wish to accept Bharatha's sacrifice, nor to consume him.

Hanuman arrived, the fire was extinguished. In all directions, sorrow turned into a boundless ecstasy of joy. Dharma whirled its head and danced.

And Vasishta hid a smile behind his moustache, in the hope that after fourteen long years, his dream would come true.

Thinking that he had no place in that carnival of happiness, Gotaman went home.

Ahalya exulted inwardly, certain that Rama and Sita would come to visit her. And they did come after the revelries had quietened down. On their own, without their retinue.

Experience had dug its channels in the brow of the Rama who stepped down from the chariot. And through experience, Sita's radiance had come into full flower. The harmony of their laughter conveyed the bliss of moksha.

Gotaman invited Rama to walk with him, and they left the house together.

With that special compassion which flows towards a child who has lain and grown in one's womb, Ahalya took Sita inside. They sat down, smiling at each other.

Sita told her everything without a tinge of sorrow – Ravana's abduction, her suffering and her release. Where was the place for sorrow, now that she had joined Rama once again?

Then she spoke of entering the fire. Ahalya was shaken to the core.

"Did he ask you to do it? Why did you do it?"

"He asked me, I did it," said Sita quietly.

"How could he ask you?" shouted Ahalya, Kannagi's frenzy leaping through her mind.

One law for Ahalya, quite another for Rama?

Was it a betrayal after all? A judgment, which was equal to the curse that had poured out from Gotaman?

For a long time they were both silent.

"Didn't it have to be proved to the world?" Sita said, laughing softly.

"If one knows it oneself, isn't that enough? Is it possible to prove the truth to the world?" demanded Ahalya. She was bereft of words.

Again she said, "And will it become the truth if you just

Kannagi is the the heroine of *Silappadikaram*, a fifth century epic by Ilango Adigal. She married Kovalan, a merchant prince of Puhar. In Madurai, where they had moved in search of a new life, Kovalan, falsely accused of stealing the queen's anklet, was put to death on the king's orders. Enraged, Kannagi arrived at the king's court brandishing the remaining anklet and clamouring for justice. She proved her husband's innocence by breaking it open and exposing the rubies inside, for the queen's anklet had contained pearls, and burned down Madurai.

Pudumaippittan

demonstrate it, even if it doesn't touch the heart? Anyway, leave it, what is this world?"

They heard voices outside. The men had returned.

Sita came out, ready to return to the palace. Ahalya was not with her.

It burnt Rama's heart. The dust spreading over his feet burnt him.

The chariot rolled forward, the sound of the wheels faded away.

Gotaman stood stock-still, lost in thought. The uncertain, impermanent constellation of Trisanku in the southern sky, fell upon his eyes.

In the cave of his mind a new thought flashed like lightning and disappeared. What if they were to have a child in order to ease their heavy hearts and revive their old attachment? Surely its tender fingers would set down her heart's burden at last?

He went inside.

Ahalya was barely conscious. In her mind Indra was re-enacting the same scene, the scene she strove to forget.

Gotaman embraced her. She thought it was Indra re-entering his role, disguised as Gotaman. Her heart hardened into stone. Stillness at last.

Entangled in Gotaman's arms lay a stone statue.

Ahalya was stone once more.

Her heart's burden ceased.

In quest of Kailasa, a solitary human form hurried across the wastes of snow. Those heels had hardened through a profound indifference to all things.

It was Gotaman. He had renounced the world.

the affairs of subbayya pillai

when subbayya pillai of Virapandyan Town first laid siege to Chennai in order to make a living, there were no electric trains, and certainly no Minambakkam airport. That example of concrete culture known as Mambalam was nothing but a marshy lake. As for Tambaram, it was a far, distant land.

In the days when Tirunelveli station was a single red building in the middle of a grove, when it was a mere intermediary stop without the prestige of a Junction, the Trivandrum Express used to come and stand there, showing every sign of weariness after a four or five hour journey past Thanjavur. At that time, if you wanted to go to Virapandyan Town, it was cheapest to travel by mail train, but quicker if you went on the big charabancs of

Lakshmi Vilas or Ganapati Vilas. The young men of Tirunelveli used to go by jutka to visit their mistresses in Srivaikundam, returning the same night, by ten o'clock. Jutkas were considered very fashionable in those days.

Sri Subbayya Pillai was a mere youth then. He had set off in the fond hope of returning with enough wealth so that he could astonish his hometown by building himself a castle. But he had never come back, except for a few lightning visits on such occasions as his own wedding, his father's death, et cetera, and when he could afford to take five or six days' leave.

Dhanalakshmi Provision Stores was initiated by a local pillai of Pavazhakkara Street, who manipulated the caste loyalty of the Tirunelveli immigrants who lived in those parts, in order to advance his business in groceries. Sri Subbayya Pillai managed various departments of the business, such as payments, accounts and sales. That is to say, he was like our state ministers, during the Montford reforms.

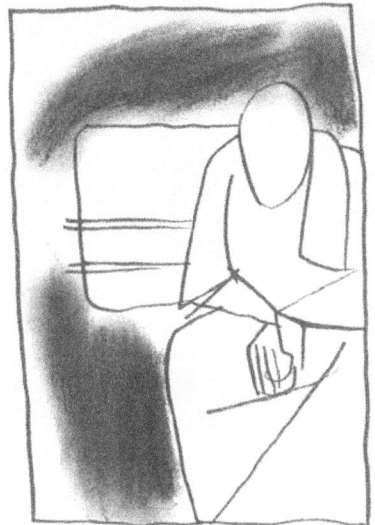

Later, Dhanalakshmi Stores turned into a clothes and textile shop, becoming a crucial link between several textile sellers of Tirunelveli's West Chariot Street, for whom it provided wholesale trade. Certainly the reason for its boom in business was the patronage it had received from the start, but one shouldn't overlook the fact that Minakshi Provision and Firewood Stores had opened just across the road.

This shop was owned by a certain Thanjavur Aiyar. His words were as sweet as sugar, personal accounts could be negotiated at his shop most conveniently. Heads of families who had accounts with him found it unnecessary even to step outside for their household needs. Yet another reason might be that the manager of Dhanalakshmi Stores began to behave in one way towards those clients who came personally to the shop because of their close connection with the Tirunelveli Saivas, and in quite another way towards those who stayed at home but sent in their shopping lists, and left their accounts in arrears month after month. And then, most importantly, a vegetarian restaurant, advertising regional Manpaanai cuisine, closed at this time. That is to say, the restaurateur pillai, who bought all his groceries at Dhanalakshmi Stores, decided to take retirement, return to his home town and live in comfort there. His son had become a revenue inspector at the Sattur Division, and it was no longer appropriate for him to be running a restaurant. He took his fare and set off to oversee his lands and property thereafter. So, for all these reasons, Dhanalakshmi Stores transformed itself into a cloth and textile shop.

Because of this change, Sri Subbayya Pillai's status rose, and so did his salary. He also gained a supplementary income through his care and attention of the Tirunelveli shopkeeper pillais whenever they visited. His clothes improved. He put aside his old handwoven, coarse veshtis, and took to wearing fine mull ones. He accumulated a little money in the bank. At the same time, his family too, grew. And although the house rent was an increasing burden on his household budget, the conveniences he gained did not match up to the money he spent.

Neither the Non Cooperation Movement, first phase of the country's awakening, nor the Salt Satyagraha that followed upon it in a great wave, made any impact upon his lifestyle, nor on his mode of thinking. He lived in Chennai exactly as if he were in a small part of Virapandyan Town. His work first of all, and after that his duty to others if at all possible and convenient, and his fear of and deference to society – these made up Subbayya Pillai's person. If the quarter anna newspapers did not reveal to him the strength of the Congress movement, then it isn't necessary to point out that his entire mental attitude stayed within the three reference points of Pavazhakkaara Street, Tirunelveli's West Chariot Street, and the Virapandyan Town of his memories.

The electric train made a huge change in his lifestyle. The Bangalore Naidu who had been an accountant at the shop during its previous history, decided to return (with all the marks of a lifetime of disappointment) to his hometown and his former life. This man owned a small house in Tambaram. Sri Subbayya Pillai had complete trust in the Bangalore Naidu's word. As a result of all this, it became Sri Pillai's destiny to make a daily journey from Tambaram to Beach. But although the entire city had become electrified, he still used the old kerosene lamps. Although water was now piped everywhere, he still drew his with a water pot and a rope.

All the money that Sri Pillai had spent thus far on house rent now went toward rail passes for himself and his eldest son, a student. At dawn, a bath in well water. A meal of leftover rice. Then with such treasures in his hand as a packed meal, his pass, the two-anna piece in the silver vibhuti container, he would set off in the direction of Pavazhakkara Street. He would return home to Tambaram on the last train with his empty tiffin carrier, his pass, the two annas in the silver vibhuti container, his hunger and anxiety. "I must get the girl married in good time. The eldest boy's examination fees have to be paid. I must drag that younger fellow, who is just sitting at home having failed, into some kind of employment. Tomorrow I mustn't put off the milkman, but pay him something at least, even if it's only a little sum."

By the time Sri Pillai finished all the proper rituals, ate his meal and sank down on the front thinnai with a yawn and a sigh of "Muruga," it was usually past midnight. And so it went on, everyday.

At about seven in the morning, just as the whistle of the Trivandrum express was heard at the outer signal, Sri Subbayya Pillai placed his foot on the steps of the Tambaram station stairway. If the ticket inspector standing opposite was a new fellow, he took his pass out, showed it, and then climbed up. Otherwise, his feet moved up along the steps while he was lost in his own thoughts, and his eyes looked searchingly towards the south, in the direction of the incoming train, in the desire and hope of seeing someone he knew arriving from Tirunelveli. It was only after the Express departed that the electric train would start. During this time, Sri Pillai took an intense pleasure in going to the platform where the Express train stood, gazing at the people who stuck their heads out in the hope of ridding themselves of the discomfort of a mosquito infested night with the aid of a swift cup of Chinglepat coffee.

Four lengths of mull wrapped around him, a coarse towel over his shoulder, the vibhuti container tied at his waist, the tiffin carrier, et cetera, in his hand – you always saw Sri Pillai with these treasures, rain or shine. A face unshaven for a week, vibhuti shining on his forehead, his hand combing out the tangles of his still wet hair – think about these things, and the very image of Subbayya Pillai will stand in front of you. In the rainy season he was usually seen with an umbrella held open in one hand, his tiffin carrier in the other.

It was impossible for the West Chariot Street tradesmen to escape him and engage in their trade directly. If they ever tried to do so, it was only because of Sri Pillai's poor health and his failure to get to the station on time. Because of this, the Manager Pillai had a special fondness for him, which, however, he did not reveal outwardly. "If Subbayya isn't around, it's as if my right hand is broken," he would say. All the same, in the matter of money, he was extremely tightfisted.

Sri Pillai climbed into the train in his own unique way. He would only sit in the compartment at the dead centre of the train, in a seat just to the right of the entrance, and always facing away from the engine. This was his special seat.

Nobody ever debated the point with him, since he boarded the train at its starting point, and left it only at its terminus. Anyway, had they attempted to do so, they could never have hoped to win. His meditation was broken only during the two minute periods when the train stopped at the various Pakkams and Pettais from Tambaram to Beach station. He never got off the train on the instant that it arrived at Beach station. And having climbed out eventually, Sri Subbayya Pillai would shake out his veshti and retie it, replace the mundu over his shoulder, thrust his head

---

Pakkams and Pettais: Neighbourhoods and suburbs adjoining a town. Chennai is made up of a conglomeration of these, linked together by the electric train.

and arm through the window and pick up his tiffin carrier, and then set forth at last, after all this. Subbayya Pillai was the last passenger to leave the station, gently, casually, at his own pace. And he was also the first to enter the train, both at Tambaram and at Beach. He never owned any such thing as a clock. He himself was a clock.

Once Sri Pillai sat down in the train, he turned towards the window, but never thrust his head outside. He sat in the very same position as if his neck had been frozen, until the moment when the fortress walls of Beach station hit his eyes. His eyes showed no signs of recognition, you could not say whether any object or any living creature was visible to him, and almost certainly he saw nothing.

The one exception to this was at Minambakkam station. As the train neared it, his eyes came alive. Startled, they looked past the park and its gravel path, and came to rest at the distant airport.

Sometime or other I will fling my money to the winds, climb into an airship and see it all for myself. This was his daily hope and prayer. Sometime or other … From the time that arrangements for a civilian airport were made known, to this very day, there never seemed a limit to that Sometime. He was a Nandan, gazing towards Thillai for the span of those two minutes, before the train moved on, towards Chennai. After that, all that was left was a quickening in Sri Pillai's bloodstream as the airport building made its appearance a moment later, only to hasten the train and its passengers on their way, while remaining behind. By the time the next station was reached, his entire mind was submerged in thoughts of Japanese cotton materials and saris. Every time his mind surfaced, there were other worries – seeking a match for his daughter, writing once more to a particular address for the balance they owed the shop, deciding that this year at least he should carry the kavadi for Lord Muruga during the month of Vaikasi ... And all the time Beach station drew nearer ... If only I could make a single trip to Tirunelveli, I could finalize the girl's marriage, make a kavadi, and even find an opening for the younger boy, all at the same time. When the Radhapuram lad was on his way to Colombo, they said they would make a proposal, it is now all of six months since his return, anyhow it might be best to drop them a letter today, before attending to anything else. If I look in on that Seth fellow and go on to the shop directly after that, I shan't need to go out again. Anyway that will be the best time to speak to the manager... It seems he too has to go out of town for a month or so ... It's all my fate ... Anyhow, I'll ask him and see what happens.

The train arrived at Mambalam and stopped. On the platform there was a huge crowd, a terrible noise. Vendors with their baskets and office clerks pushed and shoved each other without any show of discrimination, and crowded in. In all that rush, a young girl of sixteen pushed her way swiftly ahead of an old man who had just climbed in at the nearest entrance, complete with his big bundle and staff, and occupied the empty space in the bench opposite Subbayya Pillai.

She doesn't appear to be a woman. How she pushed and shoved and ran ahead to her seat! Isn't there a ladies' compartment, thought Subbayya Pillai in surprise.

The girl who had come in and sat down so confidently was a student. Clearly a medical student. A stethoscope hung around her neck, like an ornament, along with her long chain. A sari whose colour was difficult to determine, combining several shades, appropriate for the morning. A matching blouse. Her artificially curled hair had been drawn loosely over her ears and gathered into a knot. From her ears, curving silver earrings dangled. In her hand she held either a book or a notebook, he hadn't noticed carefully enough. He rubbed the palm of his hand against his forehead, because of an itching sensation there. Then, rubbing his eyes and stroking the chin which a razor had not touched for a week, he gazed through the window at the houses outside. Again his eyes returned to the bench.

The old man who had struggled with his sacking bundle had now let it rest against his knees, and was sitting by himself at the very edge of the bench, ruminating and yawning, his staff held in both hands. As for the girl, she was leaning back comfortably, and having swept a glance towards the passengers standing about in the compartment, she now opened her bag and became engrossed in looking at something there. The train began to move.

His eyes fell on the square, concrete buildings of Kodambakkam. He told himself, You can't just bear a child and then abandon her. He thought of his daughter, who was at this very moment carrying water home from the well, whose marriage needed to be decided upon. His mind refused to think of her and this girl opposite him as belonging to the same species of Woman.

As if an electric shock had gone through him, Sri Pillai drew his feet back sharply. Because of the press of the crowds, the edge of her slipper had grazed the tip of his toe. With a startled look, he drew not only his legs but his entire body within the confines of his seat, gathering himself into a tight knot. The girl glanced at him briefly and then returned her attention to the book she was holding. There had not been any intention in her glance. Yet it pulled at his heart as if with a hook. The sweat gathered upon his forehead and he looked out of the window to his right, at the fields and the heaped-up buildings.

His thoughts turned to his own marriage of long ago. The new bridegroom of Virapandyan Town. Srimati Pillai's shy and bashful form entering her new home, covered in turmeric and decorated with henna, accompanied by drums and wedding music, the day he undertook to carry the burdens of the family, bodily discomforts, chains, a blind lust when the lamps were extinguished ...

With a great clanging noise, an electric train hastened towards them along the opposite line. For a few seconds while the two trains crossed each other there was an unbearable noise jolting and confusing the ear and the mind, windows raced past, heads appeared and disappeared. At last! The train was gone. The noise faded away into the distance.

The echo of that noise pushed Sri Pillai's thoughts in a different direction ... At the corner of Broadway a tram and a car draw close, are just about to collide. The girl is caught in the middle. Sri Pillai reaches across and pulls her away, saves her life. "These things will happen if you are on your own," he tells her. He sees the girl in another place, in a rickshaw, the axle pin of the rickshaw comes apart. He runs up and takes the strain so that it doesn't fall down. Meanwhile a huge crowd gathers. He wrestles and fights his way through the crowd, saves her and carries her away. Sri Pillai's thoughts return again and again to her image ... He turned his face away, towards the window. Have we passed Egmore, he wondered, in surprise.

Park Station!

Passengers descended in crowds. When Sri Pillai looked across, the seat opposite was empty. The old man too had gone with his bundles and possession. When did the girl leave? She had arrived in haste and departed in the same haste ... But most of the crowd had left the train and gone, now. His compartment was almost entirely empty.

The electric whistle sounded.

The train started to move again. He craned his neck and looked about him. Appada! Nobody at all. He stretched his legs out on the opposite bench, rested his head against his joined hands, half closed his eyes and sank back into thought. Once again the image of the girl danced across his mind. He cracked his knuckles in front of his mouth and yawned. "Siva," he sighed.

The train passed the fort and was moving along within sight of the sparkling sea. When I leave, I must remember to make some arrangement for the milkman ... If I'm successful with the next chit, it will be adequate for the cost of a return fare to Tirunelveli ... If I place an order at Tiruchendur, at least we'll get Murugan's vibhuti every month ...

The train blew its whistle.

Should I choose a veshti for the younger boy? I bought him a couple just last month ... I need to discipline that lad.

The train came to a stop.

He climbed down, readjusted and refastened his veshti. He shook out his upper cloth and replaced it on his shoulder. He leaned through the window, picked up his tiffin carrier and set off.

The last passenger who was checked by the ticket inspector was Subbayya Pillai.

god and kandasami pillai

melakaram me ka raa kandasami
Pillaiyavargal, otherwise known as Chellappa, only son of
Melakaram Me Ka Ramasami Pillaiyavargal was standing at the
junction of Broadway and Esplanade, in a relatively safe corner,
thinking furiously. Were he to take the tram, it would cost one
anna and a quarter, leaving him with a quarter anna. He could
then buy betel leaves from the stall next to the bus stop, and walk
home, chewing blissfully. If, on the other hand, he were to board
the bus, avoid the bus conductor as far as Central, and then buy
a ticket to Triplicane, he might drink half a cup of coffee and go
home, but he would have to forego the betel leaves.

When the conductor virtually pleads with me to deceive him,

"Kadavulum Kandasami Pillayum" was first published in *Kalaimagal* in it really goes against the grain of dharma to disappoint him. Now if only I had given him the fare, exactly as he asked, just from Central onwards, I might have enjoyed a cup of coffee.

A cup of coffee right now would certainly put life into me. It was while Pillaiyavargal of the above mentioned town was engaged in such serious philosophical matters that God manifested Himself to him.

He didn't appear all of a sudden and stun him into a state of ecstasy by insisting, "Here, take this boon."

He merely asked, "Ayya, how do I get to Triplicane?"

"You could take a tram, you could take a bus, or you could walk all the way by asking passers by – The way to Madurai lies in your mouth," answered Kandasami Pillai.

"I'm not going to Madurai, I only asked the way to Triplicane, so what is the shortest way?" asked God. Both of them doubled up with laughter.

They stepped away from the jostling, shoving, pushing animated crowds and stood to one side, near a cobbler offering shoe repairs.

Melakaram Ramasami Pillai's son and heir was forty five years old. His build was that of one deprived of food for forty five years, his head was covered in grey with a sprinkling of a few black hairs, his face had not been shaven for the past two weeks, his eyes were keen enough to swoop down on his friends, however distant they were and in however dense a crowd, he wore a shirt of unbleached cotton and a veshti and angavastram of the same material.

Kandasami Pillai looked intently at the person who had asked the way. It was impossible to determine his age. He might have been sixty years old. But equally, he might have seen sixty thousand years. Anyway, he had a well setup, even opulent figure, as if he had never had to worry about his meals in all those years.

His hair, completely grey, without a single black strand in it, had not been combed nor tied back, but fell upon his neck like a lion's mane, spreading out on all sides. Right at the centre of his throat there was a big black swelling. His brilliant black eyes darted, in sharp movements, in all directions. Sometimes they drooped, as if they belonged to a madman. And his smile? At times it terrified Kandasami Pillai, at times it was like that of a fond child.

"I'm terribly thirsty," said God.

"You won't get any water-geeter here. If you want, you can have some coffee. There's a cafe over there, look," said Kandasami Pillai.

"Why don't you come with me, let's taste and see what it's like," said God. Now Kandasami Pillai was a great abedavadi. Not for him the fine distinctions between himself and the Supreme. He certainly didn't bother about the trivial differences between strangers and friends.

"Very well, come on, let's go," he said. A passing doubt went through his mind, supposing he were to be stuck with the bill? But then he resolved, Unless one dares, there's only torment.

They went into a spacious restaurant. God followed Kandasami Pillai, trailing close behind.

They sat down at a table. Without allowing the young waiter

to reel off the cafe's menu, Kandasami Pillai said, shaking his head vigorously, "Two cup coffee, hot and strong."

"Don't forget your Tamil. Say Two coffees," reminded God.

"Not so, one ought really to say two cups of coffee," said Pillai, raising the flag for Tamil.

Outmanoeuvred, God now looked about him. "This is a fine, tall building, there's a lot of light," he observed.

"Well, did you expect a restaurant to be like a hen coop? I suppose you think it's as easy as building a temple? The Hygiene Inspectors these days won't let you do as you please, you know," said Pillai, following up his victory smartly.

As soon as the word Temple fell on his ear, God began to tremble all over.

"Meaning ... ?" he asked, not willing to let go, even when he had lost. "Please explain what you mean by hygiene."

"Oh, that? It means washing down the tables with antiseptic lotion so that the inspectors don't fine you. It's also a subject that children are taught at schools, in order to make them fail exams. According to it, flies and mosquitos are equal to the rakshasas of old. If such creatures enter restaurants such as this, it's an absolute disaster. They say you cannot hope to escape with your life," said Kandasami Pillai. He himself was astounded by the turn in the conversation. He began to wonder whether the Goddess Saraswati had suddenly graced his tongue.

God didn't take much notice of him, though. He was observing a fly that was caught in a puddle of coffee spilt by a previous customer. It was struggling, flailing about, straining to free itself from the sticky liquid.

"Here we are," said God. He stretched out a finger to aid the fly. It flew away. God's finger touched the spilt coffee.

　　　　　　　　　　　　　　　　Pudumaippittan

"What are you doing, ayya, you've gone and touched someone's leavings. Here, take this water and wash your hands under the table," said Pillai.

God muttered to himself, "Mustn't allow flies to come in. Hygiene means you must wash your hands under the table."

The boy brought the Two cup coffees and placed them on the table.

God picked up his cup and drank. A divine glow spread on his countenance, as if he had supped on soma, the heavenly drink.

"Our lila, the work of the gods," he said.

"Nothing of the sort. It's not your lila, it's the restaurateur's lila. He's made it with a good pinch of chicory. Your lila will be necessary in the final chapter of paying the bill," said Kandasami Pillai in God's ear. He was delighted with himself for clearing up the matter of the bill so subtly.

"And chicory powder means ...?" God asked, raising his head, full of doubt.

"Chicory powder looks exactly like coffee, but it isn't. It's like people deceiving the whole world in the name of the Deity," said Kandasami Pillai.

When he heard the word, Deity, God was startled.

When they went to the counter to pay the bill, Kandasami Pillai was shocked as God pulled out a new hundred rupee note.

The proprietor who was at the till said, "If it was change you wanted, wouldn't I have given it to you if you had asked? Why do I have to write out a bill for three annas? To wipe my eyes or salve your conscience?"

"We really did come here for the coffee," said God.

"Surely you would have thought to keep some change ready, in that case," said the manager. But because there was a long queue waiting, of people who had just finished their meal, and because he didn't want to make trouble, he counted out the change.

"There, that's ninety nine rupees and thirteen annas. Is that right? Please check it, saami."

"If you say so, I'm happy to agree; I was never good at sums," said God.

The manager congratulated himself on having passed off a counterfeit ten rupee note.

They came out together. There wasn't such a crowd now, at the entrance. They stopped there for a moment.

God pulled out the fifth note out of the stack in his hands, tore it into shreds and flung it down.

Kandasami Pillai wondered whether the person standing next to him had suddenly gone mad. He stood there aghast, his mouth wide open.

"A counterfeit note. He tried to deceive me, but I caught him out," said God. His smile was fearful.

"If you had given it to me, I'd have caught that Pappaan by his top knot and made him change it," said Kandasami Pillai.

"You consented to drink his chicory powder, didn't you? Let's say I agreed to this in the same way. Ten rupees is a big deal to him, that's why I allowed him his deception," said God.

Kandasami Pillai was now embarrassed to abandon this stranger who had gratuitously bought him a cup of coffee.

"You're bound for Triplicane, aren't you? Come on, let's get on the tram," he said.

"Let's not," said God, "Those things make my head spin. We

Pappaan: Derogatory form of addressing or referring to a brahmin.

Pudumaippittan

could walk there slowly, couldn't we?"

"Ayya, I've been on my feet all day. I can't manage a step further. Why don't we take a rickshaw instead," suggested Kandasami Pillai. He told himself in defence, After all I'm going to show him the way, why shouldn't he pay, if he can afford to tear up ten rupee notes?

"A vehicle pulled by man? Those are the best of all," said God.

They climbed into a rickshaw. "Saami, wait a second, I'll light my lamp," said the rickshaw man.

Daylight dimmed, now there were only electric lights.

"How quickly we have struck up a friendship! I don't know who you are and you don't know who I am. That we should meet like this, right in the middle of the city's commotion ..."

God laughed. His teeth gleamed beautifully. "Never mind who I am for the moment. Tell me about yourself."

Kandasami Pillai always took a special delight in speaking about himself. Was he likely to miss an opportunity like this, when he had a captive audience within the rickshaw? He cleared his throat and began.

"Have you ever seen a medical journal known as the *Siddha Vaidya Dipika*?" he asked.

"No," said God.

"Then I take it you are not familiar with the *Vaidya Sastras*, the classical medical treatises," remarked Kandasami Pillai.

"I am familiar with them," said God.

This is really embarrassing, thought Kandasami Pillai to himself. Aloud he said, "Let us agree that you are familiar with the *Vaidya Sastras*, but that you don't know the *Siddha Vaidya Dipika*. If that's the case, your knowledge of the medical treatises cannot be complete, it has to be said. I have all the issues of the past seventeen years at home, in bound volumes. I have to insist that you come sometime and read the lot. Only then can you ..."

All the issues of seventeen years! Twelve times seventeen is two hundred and four. God quailed at the idea. A fond hope came to him. Perhaps it is a quarterly?

"The *Dipika* is a monthly magazine. The yearly subscription within the country is one rupee, two and three quarters for countries abroad. A life subscription will cost you twenty five rupees. If you become a life subscriber, you'll find it really handy. If you like, I can send it to you on trial for the first year. After that we'll consider a life subscription," said Kandasami Pillai, trying his best to persuade God.

Does he think he can force me to read all seventeen volumes, collect twenty five rupees on top of that and then drive me out? I shall never allow that, thought God. Then he asked, "Whose life, by the way?"

"Your life, of course. Not mine. Nor the journal's, it is indestructible. Even when I am gone, someone else will take it up and run it, all arrangements have been made for that," said Kandasami Pillai.

Just at that moment, the rickshaw puller slackened his pace and looked back over his shoulder.

Kandasami Pillai was afraid that if the rickshaw slowed down, the other passenger might jump down and run away.

"Why are you turning around, da? There's a car coming at you, don't crash into it. Go on, quickly," said Kandasami Pillai.

The rickshaw puller said, "What saami, are you both men or ghosts? The vehicle feels as light as the wind, as if there are no passengers in it."

"We'll also give you a fare that's as light as the wind, if you don't watch out. Go on, just pull the rickshaw," Kandasami Pillai scolded. Then he went on, "Besides, I'm also a practitioner of medicines. I only deal in siddha medicines and methods. What I make out of it just barely covers the costs of running both the journal and my family. In the current issue, I've written an article about rasakattu, the use of mercury in medicine. You see, I came across an old palm leaf manuscript which explains many rare usages."

What's this, thought God, It doesn't look as if our friend is ever going to stop. Then he asked, "How many people do you treat on an average, each day?"

"Not so many that I can brag about it. Besides, keep in mind that I make my livelihood from medicine. The illness mustn't go away altogether, nor must the fellow be finished off. It's only in that way that the patient's illness can be maintained as a means of trade. If you go for an aggressive treatment thinking it's got to be either the patient or the disease, you won't have a viable employment. The illness must come down gradually and then be cured, and at the same time, the medicine mustn't cause any harm either to the man or to the disease. That's the way of commerce. Otherwise would I have been able to run the journal for these seventeen years?" asked Kandasami Pillai.

God nodded as if he understood all this.

"Come, let me check your pulse," Kandasami Pillai went on, taking hold of God's right hand.

"What, while this vehicle is actually moving?" God laughed.

"All that depends on the vaidyan's skill," explained Kandasami Pillai.

He listened carefully to the pulse for some time, and then remarked with some concern, "The pulse rate indicates a high bile content. Are you in the habit of taking poisonous substances?"

"You really are a clever fellow. Yes, you'll find all kinds of things there," laughed God.

"Well, I've been talking away about all sorts of things. Never mind all that, Where are you bound for, in Triplicane?"

"Number seven, Office Venkatachala Mudali Lane," said God.

"Adedé! But that's my address, who did you want to see there?"

"Kandasami Pillai."

"Here's a fine thing! I'm that very person. You see, it's the Deity who brought us together. And who are you, sir? I don't think I recognize you?" said Kandasami Pillai.

"Who, I? I am God," he said, casually, taking his time. He looked up at the sky and stroked his beard.

Kandasami Pillai was startled out of his wits. God? Here?

"I came to visit the earth, I'd like to be your guest for a few days."

Kandasami Pillai spoke with agitation. "Please stay as long as you wish, I have no objection at all. Only, please don't tell everyone that you are god. It doesn't matter if others take you for a madman. Only, my wife mustn't take me for one."

Then he said to the rickshaw puller, "Just stop by the streetlight, da."

The rickshaw stopped. They climbed down.

God took a crackling clean, shining, one rupee note and handed it to the rickshaw puller.

"May you be well, saami," said the man, with a satisfied heart.

He was blessing god! Really!

Pudumaippittan

"Watch it, da. Is it your business to bless a respected elder?" said Kandasami Pillai, speaking sharply.

"What if he does," God remarked. Then he said, "You speak well, appa. It's many days since I heard such words, words so comforting to my ear and heart."

"You might have heard different words if you had given him two annas less," said Kandasami Pillai.

"Yejaman, I only care about what is just. I don't bother about what's unfair. Saami, you'll always find me sitting at that particular spot. Look out for me if you are in that direction."

"You only care about what is just! I know all about it, da. Go away, you only care about the toddy shop."

"You'd know about it, if you had run about all day in the hot sun, pulling this rented vehicle. What can I say to you? God has no eyes, he allows you to speak such words, makes me listen to them."

God burst out into loud laughter. He laughed and laughed. He was happy, at ease.

"Well, well, such is this world," said Kandasami Pillai.

"Is that all it is?" asked God.

They walked on to the house.

As they came up to the lamppost just in front of the house, God stopped.

Kandasami Pillai too stopped, and waited.

"Bhakta!" said God.

There wasn't an old man standing there.

God revealed himself in his tiger skin, his matted locks, with his deer and his axe and his crescent moon. His eyes shone with ecstatic joy. There was a smile on his lips.

"Bhakta," he said once more.

Kandasami Pillai understood it all in an instant.

"Oi, God, I'm not going to be taken in by your tricks of throwing boons at me. I know you, you'll grant me a boon and push off on your business. After that another deity is likely to come along and demand my head. I'm not such an easily fooled simpleton as to accept a boon from you and voluntarily put my head in danger. All right, so you came down to have a look at the world, you wanted to be my guest. I don't have any objection whatever, to any of that. But if you want to move around with me, then you must behave like a man, like me, in fact. You must stay within the limits of human behaviour. Now please come into my house properly, keeping in mind what I've just told you," Kandasami Pillai said.

Silently, God followed him. He thought that Kandasami Pillai's argument was fair enough. It also struck him that truly there was no answer to the question, Who on earth, in all this time, has received a divine boon and profited by it?

Kandasami Pillai stopped again at the threshold of the house. "Swami, what name should I give you? Paramasivan or Ammaiyappa Pillai?"

"Paramasivan would be right. Paramasivan the elder."

"Well then, I shall call you Appa, as if you were in the position of a father to me, please agree to this, too."

"Don't do that, appa, call me Periappa, Uncle. My property won't be in any danger then," said God, laughing. Since he had decided to act according to the ways of the world, he thought he ought to be somewhat prudent.

"So what is this wonderful property of yours?" asked Kandasami Pillai.

"Only the entire universe," said God.

"You don't need to worry, I'm not as greedy as all that." So saying, Kandasami Pillai climbed the front steps of his house.

A single lamp burning in the front room made it the sanctum sanctorum of the house. Beyond that lay the long, darkened central hall. What lay further? A small child, about four years old perhaps, was playing in the front room. Her beauty was such that it filled the onlooker with joy. Her eyes seemed to sparkle with a perpetual happiness, and for no particular reason. She stood there, pulling at her hair which hung in two rats tails fore and aft, plaited from a crosswise parting, in the old fashioned way. The banana fibre which was supposed to have been tied around the front plait had slipped, it fell into her eyes, bothering her as she bent down. She had a piece of coal and a broken tile in her hands. A ragged skirt was about her waist, falling to the knees. She had been trying to draw lines upon the floor, but had straightened up to tug at the bothersome banana fibre with both hands, as hard as she could. She wasn't successful. It hurt. As she was deciding whether she should cry or tug at it one more time, her father came in.

"Appa," she shouted, flinging her arms round Kandasami Pillai's knees. She looked up at him and asked, "What have you brought me?"

"I've only brought myself," said Kandasami Pillai.

"What's this, Appa, everyday you only bring yourself. Couldn't you at least bring some fried gram?" the child pestered.

"Fried gram isn't good for you. But look, I've brought you a thaatha."

"Is this your daughter?" asked God. He simply couldn't take his eyes off her.

Kandasami Pillai hesitated.

"Say what's in your mind. These days I'm a complete vegetarian. I only like what is cooked in a mud pot. I don't even take milk or curd," smiled God.

Kandasami Pillai said, "She is like a curry leaf sprig that sprouted long past the season, just to give us joy." Then he disappeared into the darkness, saying, "Come and sit here. There won't be any water in the tap at this time, I'll go and fetch some in a water pot."

God took off his upper cloth, shook it, and laid it down on the floor of the front room and sat down. His mind was full of a certain liveliness, and a profound peace at the same time.

He held out his arms, saying, "Come here, little one, come here you little curry leaf sprig!"

In one leap she came and clambered into his lap.

"My name isn't Curry leaf sprig, it's Valli. Only Appa sometimes calls me Darkie. Why, do you think I'm so dark?"

She didn't expect an answer. Her eyes fell on the dark swelling on the thaatha's throat.

"What's that in your throat, Thaatha, black as anything, just like a naaval fruit? I want to eat it all up." Her eyes blinked as she spoke. And now she stood up in his lap and pressed her flower-like lips into his neck. Her tiny teeth tickled him. God shivered all over.

"I feel ticklish," said God, pulling away.

"What happened, Thaatha? Did some fire-gire touch you and burn you? Look it happened to me too." She held out her finger, with a darkened scab at its tip.

"Paappa, it is really a naaval fruit. Once long ago, because a lot of people gave it to me, I accepted it and put it in my mouth.

But some others came and grabbed me by the throat demanding their share. Since then, it just got stuck there. But never mind that. Don't you have any friends who will play with you?"

"But I have this tile, haven't I, and this piece of coal? Will you come and play hopscotch with me?"

The child and God began to play.

One leg bent right back, hopping on the other, God took a flying leap.

The child clapped her hands and laughed out loud. "Thaatha, you've gone and lost!"

"How?" asked God.

She pointed out that his foot had touched a black line.

"Couldn't you have told me right at the start?" asked God.

The child asked, arms akimbo, "Should you say you'd play when you don't know the rules?"

At that moment, Sri and Srimati Kandasami Pillai emerged from the darkness, Srimati following Sri, the water pot at her waist.

"This is my Periappa from Kailasavaram. You remember, the girl from Karisangkulam was given in marriage to the son of his first cousin once removed? Can you make out who it is?"

"Oh, it's that maama, isn't it, who became a sadhu and disappeared on his pilgrimages? Welcome Maama, let me greet you," she said, and setting down her water pot, she fell at his feet, making a full obeisance. The old fashioned heavy ear ornaments, the paampadam, swung against her cheeks.

God blessed her with the words, "May you and your children live long, in good health and prosperity."

Kantimatiammai – this was Kandasami Pillai's wife's name – felt a sense of total contentment such as she had never experienced before.

God asked, as if reminding Kandasami Pillai discreetly, "Are you going to leave the sack of rice right there, in front of the house?"

"I just can't tell you how forgetful he is," Kantimati exclaimed. "I asked him a moment ago whether he had bought the rice. He said he hadn't remembered to buy it. He dispenses medicines to the whole town, only he hasn't got a medicine for his own forgetfulness. The god who created him should stand next to him and look upon him."

"I am sure he is standing by him and looking upon him," said God, putting on a rural accent.

"Well then, perhaps he should look upon him and laugh. Perhaps he'll come to his senses then."

God laughed.

God and Kandasami Pillai went towards the entrance of the house.

"I told you I didn't want any conjuring tricks," Kandasami Pillai whispered.

"No more after this," said God.

Kandasami Pillai heaved and shoved as hard as he could, the sack wouldn't shift.

"A fine young man you are!" said God laughing, as he picked up the sack and tucked it against his waist.

"No, no, you mustn't pick it up," said Kantimati in some agitation. Then, "Look here, I'm talking to you, can't you at least give a hand with it. You're just looking on and doing nothing."

"You just leave me alone, amma," said God, "And tell me where I should put it."

"Just let it lie here in the front room. Just put it down," said Kantimati, intercepting him.

By the time God and Kandasami Pillai had eaten, and returned to the stone ledge in the front veranda, it was eleven o'clock.

"What is your plan now?" asked God.

"Only to sleep," said Pillai, yawning.

The child came running up and said, "Thaatha, I'm going to lie down next to you."

"Go and ask your mother to spread out the mats and pillows," said Kandasami Pillai.

"Are you telling me to go to sleep too," asked God.

"If you are going to move around with human beings, then you must do as they do. If you don't like to sleep, just lie down quietly. Otherwise, you'll earn a bad reputation because of your goings on in the night," said Kandasami Pillai.

Kandasami Pillai sat on the floor of the *Siddhanta Dipika* office in Pavazhakkaara Street, writing out a detailed textual commentary. A commentary on *Boganathar's Treatise* was being serialized each month and published in Pillai's journal.

Kandasami Pillai wrote the final words. "And here is one final thing. To boiling water, add such medicinal plants as garudapicchu, kalluruvi, pulluruvi and umatthai which you might have to hand (garudapicchu can also be read as garudapacchai) ..." He watched the postman go past his door without coming in and muttered, "The journal won't go out today either," rolled up and put away what he had just written, and flexed his fingers.

A rickshaw came to a stop at his door. God and the little one got out. Valli was wearing a silk skirt, a paper package of sweets filled her hands.

The child jumped up and down. "Thaatha and I have been all around the zoo and the natural history museum."

"Why do they build a mansion, oi, just to house bundles of skin and bone? Are they wanting to ridicule me or what?" asked God. There was a certain severity of tone in his voice.

"Do you think people have the wit to think it through like that? No, no, they've arranged things in that way because they imagine they are demonstrating the uniqueness of creation. Let that be. Just hand me twenty five rupees, will you? I'll make you a subscriber for life. The journal must go out today."

"Who do you think you are fooling? For whose good is it supposed to be?" laughed God, referring to the subscription.

"I don't wish to accept charity, and I certainly don't want to get into debt, that's why I'm saying, let it be a commercial deal. You talk big about Goodness. In this world everything – from ghee to sesame oil – is adulterated. Don't you know that much," Kandasami Pillai hit out.

God plunged into thought.

Kandasami Pillai went on, "Anyway, let that be. You know Bogar mentions a garudapacchai, is there a medicinal herb by that name, or is it meant to be garudapicchu?"

"My responsibility lies only in creating a thing, you seem to be charging me with naming it as well. Is that fair? What do I know about it? I created you, your father named you Kandasami Pillai. So am I to be blamed for that?" countered God sharply.

"You two have been wandering about in the heat of the day and that seems to have roused your temper. Don't reprimand me and put me down on account of that. My only concern is that if you go and curse me now on a sudden impulse, then twenty five rupees might go down the drain unnecessarily."

The child meanwhile, had undone the packet and was eating the sweets. "Why are you talking to Appa, Thaatha? Just taste this and see, it's as sweet as anything."

Taking the pieces of laddu that she gave him and eating them, God said, "Paappa, the broken bits are for me, the whole laddus are for you."

The child took out a laddu, held it in her hand and thought for some time.

"Thaatha, the whole ones won't go into my mouth. But you say all the broken bits are for you. So is there nothing for me?"

God laughed and laughed. "It's all for you and only for you."

"All of it? For me?" she asked.

"Oh, yes. For you, and you alone."

"But then I won't be hungry later! Amma will beat me if I don't eat my dinner! Appa will give me lehiyam." The child was anxious.

"You are sure to be hungry. Don't worry," said God.

"It is true you bought it, all the same it is restaurant food. Bear that in mind," Kandasami Pillai cautioned.

"But I am here with you!" said God.

"Did I ever say you weren't?" replied Kandasami Pillai. A few minutes later, he asked, "How much is left of your hundred rupees, after your expenses of today?"

"Well, after I've given you twenty five, I shall have fifty rupees left," said God, smiling.

"So what do you plan to do, after that?"

"That's what I don't know, either."

"You could practise vaidyam, like me."

"I have no wish to enter into competition with you."

"Please don't think of it like that. You would not be in competition with me, but with the world's folly. Still if you don't care for that idea, you could give lectures in Siddhanta philosophy?"

"You are trying to counsel me on a means of livelihood. Would I really make any cash that way?" laughed God.

"So, what then?"

"You know, I can dance really well. What do you think? If necessary, I could contrive to have Devi with me as well."

Kandasami Pillai thought for a while. "Somehow, I don't care for the idea," he said.

"So, how else am I to survive? Come on. After all, the entire universe survives only through our dance."

"As you wish," said Kandasami Pillai. He thought for a little while longer. Then, "Come, let's go," he said, taking his upper cloth from the nail on which it was hung, shaking it out and putting it on.

"The little one," said God.

"She's fast asleep, let her be until we return," said Pillai.

A quarter of an hour later, three people entered the mansion belonging to Diwan Bahadur Brihadisvara Sastrigal. One was Kandasami Pillai, another was God. The third was a female, Devi.

"I make thangapaspam for him, medicine of gold turned into ash, on a regular basis. He'll certainly listen to me if I ask for a favour." Pillai was explaining all this at length as he climbed up the steps to the front veranda. The other two followed him. There was a small bundle in Devi's hands.

Kandasami Pillai spoke with authority to the servant. "Is saami at home? Tell him I've come to visit him."

Diwan Bahadur of affable speech, shrivelled body, fine cotton veshti and upper cloth, and gold rimmed spectacles was hastening towards them. "Oh, is it Pillaiyavargal? Please come in, come in. The powder was finished with yesterday's dose. I was getting really anxious because you hadn't turned up." The apparition greeted everybody effusively, and seated itself in an easy chair.

"Please sit down, do sit down," invited the Diwan Bahadur.

Kandasami Pillai felt his pulse and said, "Not bad, I'll have the medicine sent round this evening. But the reason for my visit is actually to introduce these two to you. Between them they are an absolute ocean of knowledge concerning the Natya Sastra. If you could arrange for them to dance in your Nritya Kalamandali, it would suit them very well."

All Diwan Bahadur's enthusiasm suddenly withdrew like a tortoise's head and feet. He joined his hands together, placed forefingers and thumbs against his nose and chin respectively and nodded his head, muttering, "Mm, mm."

"This gentleman's name is Kuthanaar, the lady's name is Parvati. They are a married couple." Kandasami Pillai explained the relationship.

"I don't recognize the names. Have you given any performances before this?" Diwan Bahadur addressed the question to Kuthanaar, but kept his gaze on Devi.

Devi answered, without giving God an opportunity to open his mouth, "There isn't a place where we haven't danced."

"Somehow it hasn't come to my notice. Never mind. But the lady appears to be very dark, it seems to me she may not show up very well to the audience," remarked the colour conscious Diwan Bahadur.

"Are you interested in looking for a bride, or did you want to see us dance?" asked Devi.

"Amma, don't be annoyed. But listen, let me tell you something. It is true there is no correspondence at all between culture and colour, except that the two words begin with the same sound. But I've been president of the Kalamandali for thirty years. I know when the eyes of the spectators darken with displeasure."

Devi made as if to go, saying, "You are welcome to keep your mandali and your sundeli."

"Please don't get angry," cried Kandasami Pillai and the Diwan Bahadur, rising to their feet together.

Once again Kandasami Pillai spoke up in their favour. "These two can dance in completely new modes. It's impossible to see such virtuosity in these parts. The Sastras themselves are put to shame by them. Why don't you see them perform, just once?"

"Very well, I'll see them perform. What objection can there be to that," and the Diwan Bahadur lay back in his chair. "Well, all right then, let them do it," he said, and shut his eyes.

Devi stood up and said, "Where's a good, wide space?"

"Why not go into the central hall?" asked God. They agreed to this, went in, and shut the doors. Within a few minutes a melody sounded, sung in a majestic voice, clear as a bell,

> *He is Rudra of the cremation ground*
> *He is Rudra ...*

The doors opened.

God stood there, still as a statue, eyes closed, clad in tiger skin, the trident in his hand, his locks of hair entwined with snakes, Ganga tumbling through them.

Once again, that music. As he turned his neck sharply, in a swift movement as if the tangles in a bolt of lightning were being shaken out, the trident in God's hand sparkled and leapt, with his eyes full of frenzy, a smile tumbling upon his lips, he raised his foot.

Kandasami Pillai was extremely uneasy at heart. Thinking that God had surely forgotten the promise he had made, he rose to his feet in his anxiety.

"Oi, Kuthanaar, stop your dance for a while."

Then the Diwan Bahadur began to remonstrate. "Chut! this is nothing more than a street performance. What's this? What sort of ridiculous costume is this, you look like the Wild Man of Borneo."

God stopped in the very pose that he had assumed, and stood leaning against his trident.

The Diwan Bahadur said, "Oi, do you know anything at all about Art? You've gone and tied a real tiger skin about yourself. Does anyone go and bring a real snake on to the stage? You should wear a snake ornament, for goodness sake! You need a piece of silk that looks like a tiger skin. The first thing you should know about Art is that it should look pleasant to the eye. Even if Parvati and Parameswaran themselves were to carry on like this, it won't be in accordance with Natya Sastra rules. This is not what the Sastras tell you to do. First take off all those snakes and put them away carefully in their basket, and then get rid of your costumes. Watch out now, this is a place where little children play."

He didn't let Kandasami Pillai get away lightly either. "Look Pillaivaal, just because you prepare certain medicines for me, it doesn't mean that I'm obliged to watch this stuff, and you certainly may not book a performance. I have to maintain a position in public, haven't I?"

Yet another quarter of an hour later, two people were sitting together at the *Siddha Vaidya Dipika* office, without Devi. The child was still asleep on her mat.

Both were silent for a while. Then, God said, "It looks as if it is impossible to survive in this world by doing the work one truly knows."

"You didn't appreciate what I told you, neither did the world appreciate what is dear to you. Well, why don't you try your hand at running Tevaram classes?"

God made a sound of repugnance, "Chut!"

"Has the world gone sour on you already?"

"Having seen you is like having seen the world," said God.

"And what of my having seen you," laughed Kandasami Pillai.

"It's all very well to grant you people boons from a distance. It's impossible to live amongst you," declared God.

"True, your sort are fit only for that," said Kandasami Pillai.

There was nobody to reply to that.

On the table lay twenty five single rupee notes, a life subscription.

Kandasami Pillai wrote in his account, "Income, Rupees twenty five, a life subscription in the name of Paramasivan Pillai the elder, of Kailasavaram."

The child sat up, asking, "Has Thaatha gone back to his hometown, Appa?"

chellammal

at that moment, chellammal's breath dropped, her pulse diminished, ceased. Chellammal became nameless, a mere corpse. In other words, Chellammal died in the presence of her husband, five or six hundred miles away from her family and relations, alone in the city.

Brahmanayagam Pillai, the sweat flowing like a river down his forehead, put away the fomentation that was in his hands and gazed at the body that had once been Chellammal.

He closed the eyes that looked as though they were half-shut. He took her hands which were lying wildly here and there, and folded them upon her chest. Her left leg lay folded somewhat crookedly. He straightened it, joined both legs, laid them down

"Chellammal" was first published in *Kalaimagal* in1943.

together. Her lips had fallen open slightly. He closed them, too. Although he knew in his heart that Chellammal had died, her death wasn't apparent to his touch. Her breath had only just left her.

A great weight slipped from his heart, bringing relief as if a burden had been lifted off his shoulders. At this parting and death, no flood of grief rose up in his heart, breaking through its dam, plunging him into distress. Only a peace of mind that one who had been his partner in this life had laid down her burden of suffering at last.

Brahmanayagam Pillai had achieved a seasoned mind. Even under the shadow of death he had not lost his balance. But it should not be assumed, because of this, that Brahmanayagam Pillai had severed all bonds of attachment, and become a yogi. His father had not been like the great and wise Suddhodana protecting him, building a fence around him, rearing him with loving care and bringing him at last to the tree of enlightenment. No, Brahmanayagam Pillai had been one who had encountered direct experiences of poverty, disease and death, all three.

To say that Brahmanayagam Pillai had seen the heights and depths of life means that the small heights he had climbed from time to time were actually false impressions in the downward

slope which gradually led into an abyss. For he had started out on the experience of life from a comparative height.

Brahmanayagam Pillai's father's progeny were so numerous that had the lands and property which provided for the family's annual income been divided, then there would have been just enough to ensure that no one need actually go hungry.

Brahmanayagam Pillai was the fourth child. Because he showed a sharpness of intellect as a youth, his father made an effort to give him a proper education. As for the others, he only cared that they should just barely read. His father's means were such as to enable Brahmanayagam to gain an education which just kept him from starvation, even though he had to travel five or six hundred miles away from home to do so. And at the proper time, Brahmanayagam had the good fortune to take Chellammal by the hand, to tread on the grindstone, and to look upon the star, Arundati, the symbol of constancy.

Brahmanayagam's father died. The property was divided. While the elder sons stayed, attempting to keep the family debts under control and not reach the stage of litigation, Brahmanayagam Pillai took Chellammal by the hand, and in order to make a living one way and another, took refuge in Chennai.

Chennai offered him a far from peaceful life, a trial by fire. Chellammal gave him an unquiet life, a different ordeal. Not because of her character, but because of her bodily weakness. She became more and more infirm. In the world outside, Pillai experienced a constant struggle. At home an ever-present and corroding anguish.

Brahmanayagam Pillai found work in a cloth shop. The manager paid him a salary which allowed the couple to keep body and soul from falling apart. Chellammal's illness, though, apart from eating up half that salary, carried them into debt as well.

The troubles that rose in Brahmanayagam Pillai's mind were at first like open wounds, but in course of time they healed, leaving only scars. There wasn't such a thing as a particular date when he was paid a salary, the custom of the shop was supposedly that he would ask for what he wanted, as and when the need arose. In practice, Brahmanayagam Pillai had to anticipate his needs, prepare the manager's mind to receive them, and then beg and plead every day without fail. At last one day, just as he made his usual request, fully expecting a rejection, his peace of mind would be shattered, and he would be given something to take home. This was the customary mode of operation at his workplace. With the shrewdness and skill of a snake that attempts to swallow its own tail, Brahmanayagam Pillai divided his needs into instalments throughout the month, but often was forced into spending his ready cash not on the needs that he had foreseen but on some unexpected emergency. Instalments were the waterways through which he channelled his meagre means of livelihood, in an attempt to irrigate the endless deserts of his wants.

Chellammal became more and more feeble. Constant mental agony and lack of food added to the illness and made her take to bed. Even the little strength she had in the morning faded away by the end of the day. Because of this, as well as reasons of thrift, Brahmanayagam Pillai chose to live in a house outside the city limits, where there were few crowds, but where there was no electricity either. Every morning he dealt with his hunger and then set off by foot, packed lunch in his hand, walking all the way to the source and means of his daily bread. He returned at last when it had grown dark, walking down the path that led to his front door at an hour when all other workers had already had their dinner and were ready for bed. His meal depended entirely on the condition in which Chellammal had spent the day. If, when he came home, he found the house dark, the outside door shut but not bolted, it meant that unless he went inside, washed his hands and feet with all customary rites, and then lit the hearth, there was no other way for the two people to fill their bellies. Since all the shops in that vicinity were closed at that time, he would have to manage with what there was already in the house. Sometimes what was available was only the treasure of empty, shining vessels. Even at such a time, Pillai never lost his even temper. He would, at the very least, prepare some hot water for his wife.

And so, Brahmanayagam Pillai spent ten years in Chennai in this fashion. The daring thought had struck him, certainly, from time to time, that they should return to his village. But the next minute, his own powerlessness bound him down with a profound disappointment and bitterness. Besides, he was also terrified at the thought of how things had turned out there.

Sometimes he had talked about ways and means by which they might relieve themselves of their troubles with that corpse lying there now, when life throbbed through it, talked of pleasures yet to come, should they make off home to the village. Sometimes Chellammal would laugh with sudden enthusiasm, causing her dry lips to split. Memories, to the couple, were like ganja, or some other intoxicating drug, a convenient means to make them forget present anxieties.

That day, as Brahmanayagam Pillai stepped across the front steps with his packet of leftover rice, Chellammal had been able to get up and move about. Having told him that she intended to cook his favourite horse gram relish and make a sour curry with tamarind in it so that he could eat a meal that was to his liking that evening, she went off to the back of the house, charcoal and ash in hand.

Brahmanayagam Pillai turned round from the threshold to warn his wife, "You've just this morning been able to lift your head and get about a little. Don't overdo it unnecessarily." Then he pulled the door shut from outside, steadied it with one hand while cleverly inserting a finger through the narrow space between the door and its frame in order to draw the bolt. Then he pushed the door once again to make sure the bolt had slipped into place properly, before stepping into the street and walking away.

All along the way to work his thoughts circled around how receptive the Store Manager's state of mind might be, and about Chellammal's heartfelt wishes.

The night before last, during the course of conversation, and while he was giving her a hot fomentation to relieve a chest pain, Chellammal had spoken to him about it. "I long to eat our home-grown rice at the next Pongal festival. Let's go home this once. When we come back we could bring some nellikkai adai, and a measure of dried murungakkai."

Her words sounded fair enough. But she might have asked him to fetch her some tiger's milk, she might have asked him to acquire some impossible skill, they would not have been unattainable dreams by comparison.

"Why not? Of course, we'll see. The month of Purattasi isn't over yet, it's only after it's passed that we need to plan for Pongal."

"True enough, but we've got to tell Them now, don't we, so that They can arrange it?" said Chellamma explaining the urgency. They referred to the store manager Pillai.

"At any rate, you don't have to worry about Deepavali, everything will come from the shop," she went on. "And what do I get this year?"

"Oh, I'll pick up something that I am sure will please you, that's easy. But first you should be well enough to lift your head and sit up," smiled Brahmanayagam Pillai.

But all along the way he kept wondering to himself, "What can I write in the account book, and what can I bring her? As it is, I haven't paid up my arrears. How will they allow me to keep on adding to my expenses?" He entered the shop and put away his tiffin carrier and his upper cloth in the corner reserved for him.

"What is it dé, Brahmanayagam? Why so late? Who did you think would come and open the shop? How are they at home? Yes, yes, well, go upstairs and bring down half a piece of 703. And while you are about it, there's a stack of banians in the north corner, bring that as well." The commands of the manager drew him into the routine operations of the establishment. And Brahmanayagam Pillai dashed about, worshipping the God of the Stomach with a laksharchana, chanting a hundred thousand times, one yard, half a yard, coloured yarn, Salem Kollegal, poplin, twill.

At last, at nine at night, he mentioned his needs to the manager with great hesitancy, took three saris on approval, made a record of them, wrapped them up in his upper cloth, and set off for home.

Brahmanayagam Pillai arrived at the threshold of his house, set down his bundle, and, as usual, slipped his finger through the gap in the doorway and drew the bolt. In the street, a dog which had been swallowed up by the darkness, howled aloud in distress. Its yearning cry rose up, wave upon wave, and then faded.

Brahmanayagam Pillai pushed the door open and went in.

There was no light in the house. He thought to himself, She must be asleep. After all, it's so late ... took the match box from its niche in front of the house, and lit the chimney lamp. It was like a glow worm, making the darkness gather densely. The dim light caused the shadow of his body to play monstrously on the wall.

He crossed the front room and went further inside. Chellammal lay on an outspread sari, turned towards her left side, her head upon her folded arm. Her right hand had fallen back, limp. The way she lay made him realize she wasn't just asleep. Brahmanayagam Pillai bent over her and looked directly into her face in the lamplight. Her eyeballs had rolled right up. Only the slightest movement in her chest, her breath a mere thread.

He straightened himself and went to the backyard. On his way, he glanced towards the kitchen. The food had all been prepared, and laid out in order. Hot water was boiling on the hearth.

Without haste, he pulled water from the well and washed his hands and feet. He went inside once more, took the small, shallow oil lamp by the side of the kitchen hearth, pinched out the wick and lit it. He took a piece of dried ginger and the box of matches from the niche nearby, and returned to the inner rooms.

He lit the pedestal lamp next to the wall, and came and sat down by Chellammal once more. Her hands and feet had grown cold. He poured some camphor oil into the palm of his hand, rubbed a little to warm it, and held its pungent smell towards her nose. No use. Somewhat anxious now, he poured out some more oil and smeared it on her nose and cheeks. Then he got up, brought some boiling water in a vessel, and placed a hot compress to her hands and feet and chest. No use in that either. He burnt the dried ginger in the flame of the lamp and brought the smoke to her nostrils.

Because her face had fallen to a side, it wasn't easy. Gently he rolled her over and made her lie straight on her back. Once again he brought the dried ginger to her nose.

At the second attempt, when the smoke blew at her, Chellammal moved her head very slightly to avoid it. She gave a loud sneeze which seemed to shake her entire body, and then fainted again. When the smoke blew at her once more, Chellammal muttered and then cried like a small child, calling for water.

"Here, open your mouth a little," he said, bringing hot water in a little tumbler, and trying to wet her mouth. Before he could succeed, the teeth clenched. She lost consciousness.

Once again, Brahmanayagam Pillai resorted to the remedy that had so far, in his experience, been successful.

Whimpering, Chellammal came to herself and was wide awake. Her eyes rained questions, as if she was not aware where she was.

"When did you arrive? Where's Amma? How long must I wait for you, with a meal all ready?" she asked.

Brahmanayagam Pillai was expert at answering such questions, and helping, gently, to pull back her consciousness from where it had fled. There was no need to give the correct answers to her questions, it was enough to give appropriate ones.

Suddenly, Chellammal reached forward, held his hand, and began to shout at the top of her voice, "Amma, Amma, let's go home. If that traitor comes here, he'll catch hold of me and tie me up. Traitor ... traitor ... traitor." She screeched out the words. Brahmanayagam Pillai dipped a piece of cloth in cold water with his left hand and placed it on her forehead.

Chellammal began to prattle unintelligibly. She could not recognize who was in front of her. "Amma, Amma ... When did you come? Did they send you a telegram?" she asked.

"Yes, yes, I've just arrived. There was a telegram. How are you feeling now?" Brahmanayagam Pillai asked, acting as if he was her mother. It was now five years since Chellammal's mother had died. But always, when she began to be delirious like this, she would imagine that her mother was still alive.

"Amma, give me a little water ... He's always like this, Amma ... He always leaves me alone and goes off to the shop ... When shall we go home? ... Who tied up my hands and feet like this? ... I won't ask for a sari ever again, please don't tie me up ... I'll crawl home to the village, slowly, slowly. Ayyo, please let me go ... What did I ever do to you? ... Please, won't you untie me? ... I'll just see my mother and come back ... you can tie me up after that."

Once again Chellammal lost consciousness.

Brahmanayagam Pillai wondered whether he should go and fetch the vaidyan. "But how am I to leave her alone in the house like this? Is it a short distance I have to go, after all?"

He used the dried ginger yet again.

Her pulse was beating very gently.

A fear that Chellammal might die began to stir lightly in Brahmanayagam Pillai's mind.

In that fear there was no terrible agony, nor an unspeakable grief. Only a bitterness of taste such as invalids feel upon the tongue, and somewhere beyond that, a kind of peace. A certain dismay that however hard one has tried, nothing has been gained.

Chellammal, still whimpering, lay down again, face to one side.

Brahmanayagam Pillai was putting a hot compress to her feet in an attempt to warm them and couldn't understand what she said. Before he could turn around to face her, asking, "What do you want," she began to breathe properly again. She finally came out of her fainting fit, and fell asleep. The desolate look of illness dimmed, and left her at last.

Ten minutes had not quite passed, she was awake again. She felt herself all over, wondering why she was wet, and began to gather together her scattered thoughts.

"My head aches," she said, still whimpering.

"I ache all over," she said, gently closing her eyes.

"Go to sleep quietly, without worrying yourself, you'll be all right in the morning," he said.

"Mm," she agreed and shut her eyes, but then she sat up, saying, "My mouth feels dry."

"Don't get up, you'll fall over," he said, supporting her back and giving her hot water in a tumbler. She felt its lack of warmth and said, "I don't want that. Give me some cold water, please. My mouth is so dry."

He tried to warn her, "You shouldn't drink cold water, hot water is best for you." But he decided that rather than arguing with her and upsetting her, it was best to let her have the cold water, so he poured some out for her, and then laid her down gently.

She shut her eyes for a few seconds, then said, "What about you? When did you come home? Did you eat your dinner?"

"I've eaten. You sleep now. Don't keep thinking of one thing after another," said Brahmanayagam Pillai. His answer fell on her ear but not on her consciousness. Chellammal fell asleep.

When Brahmanayagam Pillai at last spread out his rush mat against the front door, yawned and sighed, "Muruga!" and sat down, a cock crew. The world awoke. Pillai wasn't allowed the time, even to lie down a little. He sat up, with his arms around his knees. Only his thoughts touched, and then leapt about among many old, unconnected memories.

Dawn began to break. Voices of women engaged in the vegetable trade, carrying loads upon their heads, other voices of those who had progressed a bit and were riding handcarts which they would fill up later – these drove Pillai away from the distant temples of memory. He went in, bent over and observed her. She was in deep sleep, her cheek sheltered in the crook of her arm, her lips pushed to one side.

He thought it would be good to give her something to warm her belly as soon as she woke up, and so he went into the kitchen, lit the fire and then went into the backyard.

As he returned and applied vibhuti to his forehead saying, "Muruga" Chellammal woke up, sat up in bed, shook out her hair, smoothed it, tied it up and looked towards the kitchen.

Pudumaippittan

"How do you feel now?" asked Brahmanayagam Pillai, "It looks as if you slept well."

"I feel terribly weak, I ache all over as if I've been flogged. And I'm hungry. I wouldn't mind something really hot," said Chellammal, lowering her head a little, scratching her crown and wrinkling her forehead.

"There's some jaggery-coffee on the hearth that I've just made. Why not clean your teeth and have it? Shall I give you some hot water to clean your teeth?"

"Just put some hot water for me by the back door. I'll go and wash," said Chellammal.

"A fine thing to say. Have you forgotten the state you were in last night? No getting up and moving about now."

"What's the matter with you, you don't seem to care about what's dirty and what's not." Saying this, she gathered up her clothes, fastened them, and stood up. Her legs buckled.

Breathing harshly, she leaned against the wall with both hands. Brahmanayagam Pillai instantly leapt towards her and held her by the shoulder.

"Just help me gently to the back door. Let me clean my teeth. I can't seem to be able to stand up," she said.

He let her have her own way, supported her to the backyard and helped her sit down.

Having cleaned her teeth, she came and lay down once again, with several sighs of "Appada" and "Ammada." By this time she was utterly worn out. As soon as she lay down, she closed her eyes in weariness.

Pillai brought the coffee, having cooled it, and said, "It's just at the right temperature, drink it up now, don't say it's gone cold." She couldn't reply to that. She merely gestured, Let it be.

A few minutes later she opened her eyes. With difficulty she leaned against her hands and sat up. She touched the tumbler and said, "But it's not hot at all. Are there any live coals in the hearth? Put it on them for awhile."

"Leave it where it is, there is some more, good and hot. Let me bring it to you," he said, bringing her fresh coffee in another vessel.

Chellammal accepted it, held it against her chest and warmed herself, then drinking it gradually and slowly, by the mouthful, asked him, "What did you eat?"

"There was some leftover rice. I ate a handful. Drink your coffee quickly, it's getting late. I'll go and fetch the vaidyan," he said.

"I don't need the vaidyan nor anyone else. What's wrong with me now? Don't burn your money unnecessarily. I feel like eating something sour. That dosai batter which had gone sour – what did you do with it?" she asked.

"Soured batter indeed! Nonsense! Just drink up your coffee and lie down now. I'll go and find the vaidyan and bring him home with me. It seems you've totally forgotten the state you were in yesterday." He rose to his feet.

"Why are you wasting that other coffee? Why not drink it yourself?" Chellammal called after him.

Brahmanayagam Pillai, in search of a vaidyan, at last found a practitioner of siddha vaidyam, looking like a famine victim, and brought him home. When they entered the house together, Chellammal was not in her bed.

From the kitchen came the sizzling sound, srr ... srr ..., of dosais cooking. Pillai spread out a mat, invited the vaidyan to sit down, and went in search of her, muttering, "She just won't listen, in spite of everything I say. Is she a small child or what?"

Sweating all the time, Chellammal was engaged busily in what was beyond her strength. The dosai batter had spilt because her hands trembled so much. A single dosai lay on a platter, part burnt. In the fond hope that the next one would come out right, she watched the dosai griddle, oil, chili powder and all the rest of the ingredients ready to hand. She looked up at him directly, and laughed.

"Enough, enough, don't laugh. The vaidyar is here. Get up now," he said, holding her arm and lifting her up.

"Let me take this off the griddle and come."

"No, you get up now," he said, removing the griddle, along with the dosai cooking on it, and putting it aside, with its spatula.

"You go on first, I'll come," she said, and then, rearranging her clothes properly, she followed him with faltering steps and came to sit on the mat.

The vaidyan examined her pulse. He asked her to put out her tongue, and observed it as well.

"Amma, when you are as ill as this, you should never get up and walk about. Your body has become extremely weak. You're not even able to digest anything that you eat. Now for three days, your diet has to be just milk and kanji. After you have gained a little strength, I can prescribe a medicine. Don't drink coffee for the next few days. Take only milk in the morning and at night. In the afternoons, let it be gruel. You must never get up, or leave your bed. Ayya, if she starts to faint, mix this sinduram in honey and place it on her tongue. Rub this ointment on the bridge of her nose and her temples. I'll come back in three days." The vaidyan accepted a rupee for his medicine, and left.

"You went and found a fine vaidyan! He says I must have only milk kanji. Ai! Have I got some sort of a disease? Do I need a vaidyan to come and tell me my body is weak? If you are a human being, you are bound to feel faint sometimes. If it comes, it goes away too," said Chellammal.

Just then a voice was heard, calling from outside the house, "Ayya, Ayya."

"It's Munuswami, is it? Come in. I suppose they sent you to find out why I hadn't turned up at the office. My wife isn't at all well, her survival yesterday was like being granted a new birth. Please tell them I'll try to come tomorrow if I can. And Munuswami, would you do me a favour? You know the cattleshed in the next circle? You'll find a certain milkman Naidu there. Please bring him here. Tell him I need him."

Chellammal said, "Don't make me an excuse for not going to the shop. Go and earn your salary."

"Adedé, I forgot entirely. Yesterday I brought some saris home on approval. See which one you like. We'll send back the ones you don't want," he said, bringing the bundle to her.

"I saw that bundle first thing in the morning. I meant to ask you about it, but forgot completely," she said, taking the three saris out of the bundle and turning them over and over.

"I like the green one the best, what does it cost?" she asked.

"Why should you worry about that? Just choose what you like," he said, as he took the green sari and put it away in the almirah, and tied the other two into a bundle which he placed against the wall.

"Don't go and throw away good money, and then stand about rolling your eyes. I'm warning you now," Chellammal said, trying to sound severe.

Pillai arranged with milkman Naidu for the delivery of the

best cow's milk for three days. Then he sent Munuswami away with the two saris, and with a request for a loan of fifteen rupees, to be brought to him later.

From the moment she laid her head down on her mat that day, Chellammal's state of health worsened all the time. She grew more and more weak. Because he was busy looking after her at midday, the milk kanji had cooled into a paste-like consistency, so he added some hot water, mixed it, and tried to feed her with it. But she was so weak, and the food disgusted her so much, she brought it up immediately. The nausea wouldn't go away. Chellammal tried hard to eat slowly and by the mouthful. She had become so feeble though, that all her former disorders kept returning.

Although Brahmanayagam Pillai sat by her side, massaging her arms and legs until his own arms were worn out, Chellammal lay in a faint by three in the afternoon, overcome by weakness. She herself began to be alarmed, now, that she might die. Now and then she suffered from muscular cramps and shortness of breath.

"I feel so strange. Perhaps it would be best to see a different vaidyan," said Chellammal.

"It's because your body is so exhausted that you are feeling like this. But you won't lie down quietly, without moving about, as you are told to. Don't be afraid, everything will be all right," comforted Brahmanayagam Pillai.

But in his heart of hearts, he too feared the worst. "The milkman will be here soon, I'll collect the milk and then go and fetch the doctor. Should I write to Kunathur Athai and ask her to come?"

"What's the point of writing to her? How can she travel such a distance on her own? Will you make me some hot jaggery-coffee? At least it will stop this nausea."

"Here, put this sour mango stone in your mouth. I'll make you some coffee," he said, hurrying towards the kitchen.

And just as he had stirred the embers alive, and placed a pot of water on the hearth, the milkman too arrived.

He placed the jaggery coffee next to Chellammal, boiled the milk, and poured some of it out into another vessel, and set off saying, "I'll go and fetch the doctor now."

She said, without opening her eyes, "Come back soon. I'm feeling very unwell again." She was exhausted to that extent. The creaking of the front door announced that he had left.

By the time he returned, it had grown dark. He had waited and waited at the door of a paltry LMP (Licenced Medical Practitioner), expecting his return. There were no signs of him though. His imagination magnified his anxiety several times, so at last he returned home, after leaving a letter explaining the state of affairs, giving his address, and pleading with the LMP to come at once.

When he opened the door and entered the house, he was shocked by what he saw. Chellammal had fainted in the inner courtyard. The coffee she had drunk had been thrown up and lay splashed everywhere.

He lit the lamps in a hurry. He brought some hot water and washed away the vomit on her, and then carried her to her bed and laid her down.

He mixed the sinduram which the vaidyan had left, in honey, and placed it on her tongue. He rubbed the ointment on her nose, hands and feet. She did not regain consciousness. Her breath was a mere thread. He massaged the ointment more generously upon her in an attempt to bring her out of her faint.

A rickshaw arrived at that moment, and stopped outside. A doctor came in, carrying his small suitcase and his poverty, calling out, "Saar! Who's at home?"

"You came at the right moment, Ayya," Brahmanayagam Pillai said, welcoming him.

"What's happened now?" asked the doctor, as he came up and sat next to Chellammal, reaching for her pulse. He tried to open her mouth. Her teeth were clenched.

"If you've got a box of matches, please bring it here, I have to give her an injection," he said.

Brahmanayagam forgot about the box of matches in the niche, and ran into the kitchen. The doctor, waiting for his return, looked up towards the roof and saw the matches there. He picked it up, lit his spirit lamp and sterilized the needle he would use for the injection. He asked Brahmanayagam Pillai, who now appeared, matchbox in hand, dripping with sweat and foolishness, to hold up the lamp with his left hand, and injected the medicine into her. For a couple of seconds they watched her intently.

Chellammal began to moan.

The doctor collected his instruments and put them away in his case, quietly. "Let me have some shikakai powder, if you have any," he said. Brahmanayagam Pillai brought him a piece of the white soap that they used for washing his veshtis. The doctor washed his hands silently and then said, "It looks as if she is asleep. Don't disturb her now. When she wakes up, give her only milk. It's not convenient to keep cases like this at home, Ayya, hospital would be best." And saying this, he picked up his case and began to walk off.

Brahmanayagam Pillai followed him out deferentially and asked, "How do you find her?"

"Can't say there's anything to worry about now. In any case, come and tell me how she is tomorrow morning. Then we'll see. Give this rickshaw puller a four anna coin." He climbed into the rickshaw as he said this. The small change was transferred from Brahmanayagam Pillai's lap to the human animal's lap. He stood for a while, watching the rickshaw, and then went back inside.

Chellammal was asleep.

Brahmanayagam Pillai came and sat by her soundlessly, and kept on watching her. He was afraid she might wake up if he just touched her.

A fly came and sat upon her chest. It didn't care to sit for long on the soft material. It flew off again, circled, and alighted on the palm of her hand. Once again it flew off and then circled about as if it could not decide where to sit. At last it came down upon her lip.

Spitting out vehemently, "Thoo, thoo," and rubbing her lip with the back of her hand, Chellammal sat up.

For some time she looked at him intently.

"You don't have the slightest sympathy for me. How could you have left me like this and gone away?" she scolded him.

He stroked her cheek saying, "Should you have got up and walked about when I was not here?"

"It seems I really will die. Don't make a big fuss, unnecessarily," she said, closing her eyes.

"It's because you are so tired that it seems like that. Shall I press your legs for you?" And he gently massaged them.

"Appada. I ache all over. I feel a chill coming on, right inside me. Hold my hand and stay close to me." Chellammal clasped his hand in both hers, shutting her eyes again.

After a pause she said, still with her eyes shut, "I feel I really must see Amma."

"So what, I can just send her a telegram tomorrow, no problem there," Brahmanayagam Pillai assured her. Terror seized him. Was her consciousness going off the rails again?

"Mm. Don't waste your money. If you send her a letter it will do. Where's she going to come, anyway? You must go to the shop tomorrow, at least," said Chellammal.

"You just lie there quietly, without fretting." He freed his right hand from her clasp and stroked her forehead.

"It hurts. I'm thirsty. Some hot water," she asked.

"Hot water will upset your stomach, you've just been vomiting," he said. He took hold of both her hands and looked closely at her face. Since the morning her face had lost its brightness and faded. Her lips looked somewhat blue. She licked her lips frequently to stop them from drying up.

"My heart is beating in such a strange way," she said, again.

"These are all just symptoms of your weakness. Don't be afraid." He rubbed her chest for her.

A moment later Chellammal said, "I'm hungry, give me some milk. I'll go to sleep."

"I'll bring it to you right now," said Brahmanayagam Pillai, hurrying into the kitchen. The milk had curdled and gone sour. He was stunned. In the niche above, he found a single dried up lime. He squeezed it into hot water, added sugar, brought it with him and sat down by her side. He cooled the hot drink until it was at the right temperature.

"Chellamma," he called softly.

No reply. Her breath came quietly.

"Chellamma, the milk has curdled. I've brought you a sweet drink. Drink it up and go to sleep."

She nodded her head very gently as if to say, "Very well."

He poured some of the liquid into a small tumbler and took it to her mouth. She drank two mouthfuls and then shook her head.

"Why ... is the light ..." Her whole body convulsed and shuddered as she coughed. Her chest heaved and fell. Her arms and legs jerked in spasms.

When all the agitation ceased, Brahmanayagam Pillai offered her the drink again. It flowed down both sides of her mouth.

He put the tumbler down quietly and touched her.

Only the body was left.

Leaving his hand there, he looked up to see, there on the wall, his monstrous shadow. Its hands looked as if they dug into Chellammal's chest and plucked out her life.

He tried rubbing on her body what remained of the ointment that the siddha vaidyan had left. As soon as he realized it was of no use, he tried a hot fomentation of bran.

The sweat from his forehead dropped upon the body and into its eyes.

He closed the eyelids properly upon the half open eyes. He straightened the legs which had jerked upwards. He folded the hands upon her chest.

As he sat there silently, the sound of boiling water fell upon his consciousness, summoning him.

He went in and cooled the water to the exact heat at which Chellammal liked her bath.

He brought her body there. He thought, Chellammal isn't so heavy, still I can hardly carry this weight.

The head wouldn't hold up, it kept drooping to one side.

He sat her up, laying her against his legs and knees as he stood above, and used the entire brass pot of water to bathe her. He didn't know where the turmeric was kept, so he couldn't use it. He dried the body with his upper cloth.

Again he carried her back and laid her on her bed. He took the green sari that he had bought for her and wound it about her body. He put vibhuti and kumkumam on her forehead. He lit the pedestal lamp and placed it beside her head. He remembered the frankincense bought for a Saraswati puja ages ago. He brought some hot embers and sprinkled the incense upon them. He placed a full measure of paddy beside her.

He attended to all the sacred rites due to Chellammal's body, and stood for awhile, looking at it.

He felt suffocated there, in the inner room of the house. He came to the front of the house and stepped out into the street.

A fine breeze stroked him.

Among the stars that lay scattered and splashed across the sky, he distinguished the Trisanku constellation. He didn't know astronomy. The foot of the sankumandalam was caught in the distant, darkly etched temple tower, and swung helplessly, unable either to rise or set.

Near him, Munuswami's voice said, "Ayya."

He handed him some notes. "The manager sent this. How is Amma now?"

"Amma is lost to us. Hold on to this note, I'll write out a telegram. Take it to the post office, and then please go and tell the shop manager's family. When you return, please inform the barber as well."

He spoke quietly. In his words there was no sound of anguish.

Munuswami, taken by surprise, ran with the telegram.

Brahmanayagam Pillai came back into the house and sat down. He sprinkled some more frankincense on the embers.

Once again the fly circled the face of the corpse, and sat on it.

Brahmanayagam Pillai used a hand fan gently and continuously to drive it away, to keep it from alighting.

Outside, in the dawn, a double conch began its dirge as if to hide the deceit of a woman who raises a lament without knowing true sorrow in her heart.

rope serpent

what if it is an obscure village,
Kallipatti? What if it is Kailasapuram with its distinguished
address? Like the waters of the Ganga, Time, the river of life,
flows endlessly past both places. And it will go on flowing,
forever. The days we imagine and number as Sunday, Monday,
Tuesday, like a curd seller who makes marks on the wall – are
all the very same, fundamentally. Time is like a fine thread
being pulled out without a break, and without knotting. No,
no. It keeps lengthening by itself, like the thread that the spider
spins from its belly. Today, yesterday, tomorrow – these are all
nothing but convenient dreams that we build around ourselves,
for we ourselves are their primary source. The notion of an "I"

"Kayittraravu" was first published in *Kadambari* in 1948.

and following that, our understanding of difference, of all that is "not-I." The lines we ourselves have determined and drawn between "before-me" and "after-me" ... How long will these stand firm? This civilization is, after all, a string of several, separate atoms of what I myself have thought, think now and will think in the future. What is this civilization but a dolls' house made of mud which we have built because of our instinctive yearning for collective living, and by the joint straining of our thoughts? Nothing but a dolls' house built of mud on the shores of the river of life which springs from the belly of the spider called Mahakalam ... Oh well, what a beautiful fantasy. These were the thoughts of Paramasivam Pillai as he squatted down at the foot of a palmyra tree at midday.

The heat of the sun attacked the top of his head where it had escaped from the thin towel that he had twisted once around it. He shifted to a side in the shade, still squatting, and leaned over, so that the sun's rays would not fall on him. Wild bushes with their thorns and sharp edges pricked his thighs. He moved away to another side. Although his mind was bent on a universal journey, as he sat there, leaning over and gazing downwards, it was a tapeworm dead among the faeces that drew his attention.

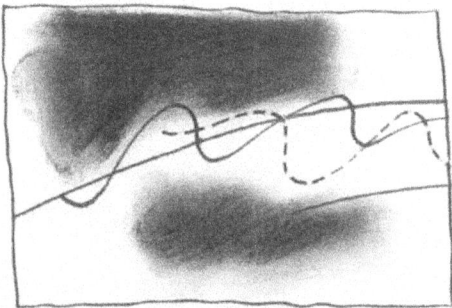 Dung-creature ... many lives, many deaths ... chichi. Revulsion overcame him and he went and sat down under another palmyra tree. It was a young palm. Because it was not too tall, its shade fell comfortably. And there were no prickling

Pudumaippittan

thorns. The stones were sharp, though.

Only his mind, unable to be at peace, returned again and again to fall upon and suffocate among the needs of the body, just like that tapeworm.

Is the mind something that can function on its own, apart from the body, without needing a body? Or is it like music, for which the vina is necessary? Before I was born ... could I have been conscious of myself? What is around me, what is about me now, does it have a consciousness?

The palmyra tree, and this little palm are both within my conscious understanding. I knew when this one sprouted. I knew the bare, hard earth which was here before it sprouted, when even this shade was lacking. Then, there was that palmyra which fell over in the winds, last Adi. Now the earth there stands bare and dry, and it is impossible to say where it once stood. There was a time before I was born ... Then, a person named Paramasivam Pillai, a creature with likes and dislikes, desires, sorrows, anxieties, learned to play with skill those games that have come down from generation to generation, and he played those games, whether he liked them or not ... Later, Paramasivam will seem only an illusory appearance, having left behind just a name as a signpost, vanishing away along the way he came, or in another direction ... A puppet show! Yet how to say with certainty that it is a puppet show? Do the strings pull themselves, or is there a puppeteer? How is it possible to say out of the two, whether it is so, or is not so? The only two things we know are the threshold through which we come, and the direction in which we go. We arrive through a birth canal, and we depart through another. Is it to our mother, Prakriti, Nature herself, that we go? Is human existence only a path that takes us from womb to womb? Is it an endless miracle?

Or a unique deception, without precedent?

As he sat under the palm tree by the shores of Kailasapuram's river, Paramasivam Pillai, imagined – with difficulty – a time when there was no "I."

Nearly half a century ago in Kailasapuram, the sun rose and set everyday, as always. In those days, there were not so many buildings of lime and plaster along the path leading to the river. There wasn't so much dust either. There was the comforting shade of marudam trees. Cattle rested there. It almost seemed as if the entire human civilization of that region too, sat there chewing cud. Yet, of course there was movement, too. Sunday ends and Monday begins. Can anyone say with certainty, at what instant? And it is the same, whether it is the clock that we ourselves have wound that tells us it is Monday, or whether we say it. So, just as what was Sunday has become what we call Monday, so too what seemed like a civilization that merely sat and chewed cud was also after all, an illusion. How, if it had just sat there, had the lime and plaster buildings sprouted? There would only have been the shade of the marudam trees, always. So the wind blew, rains fell, the river flowed in spate. The palm trees keeled over, became firewood, became crossbeams. Young palm shoots sprang up. Sunrise ... Sunset ... Azhagiyanambiya Pillai washed his veshti against the stone steps leading down to the river. He squatted down and scrubbed the dirt away. He dived into the river and bathed. He stood up and placed the sacred ash on his forehead. He performed all the appropriate daily rituals. The shade from the marudam trees fell on the stone steps. Now, though, the steps have slid down. There is a path. Water runs over the sand, hiding the protruding and scattered stones. Now there are no marudam trees. There is the heat of the sun. The stones are slippery ...

On a certain day, fifty years ago, living waters flooded a certain womb. Of the endless, million seeds growing in the waters, only one stood stable. Should we say that it alone was fortunate, out of all those million atoms of life? Or did it stand firm, with a complete consciousness of what it was doing? In any case, if it were not this atom, it would have been another. It stayed, it became individual, it took form, it gained feeling. It became a fish. It became a frog. It lost its tail. It became a monkey. In a state of supreme meditation, it slept. It became a baby. It laid its thumbs within the palms of its little hands, enclosed them within its fingers and waited, like a little bundle ...

In Kailasapuram, the trees budded. Flowers blossomed. Honeybees began their traffic. The trees grew fertile. Young fruit appeared.

Northwards from the womb there was an outcry, a prolonged howl from the stomach. A voice sounded, born out of pain. A piece of flesh fell out, head first, holding its in-folded thumbs. A new birth. It became conscious. Its organs began to work. The new life screamed. It jerked its arms and legs, fluttered its fingers, and cried out loud. They scissored away the cord that held it to the womb. It became a separate life. Acquired its own nature. It fed from the breast ... slept ... cried ... tasted the breast again.

In Kailasapuram the trees fruited, cluster upon cluster. Bunches of fruit hung down, richly green. It seemed that year's yield would pull the entire tree down to the ground.

Azhagiyanambiya Pillai sits in a moonlit terrace, holding a baby and playing with him. The baby coos to him in return.

"Who is Appa?" asks Azhagiyanambiya Pillai.

The baby taps himself on the chest, in reply.

"Idiot child, I am your appa, da. You are Paramasivam … Paramasivam Pillai," says Azhagiyanambiya Pillai.

"Who is Appa?" he asks again.

The baby touches his chest in reply.

"And who is Paramasivam?" asks Azhagiyanambiya Pillai.

"Me," says the baby, tapping himself on the chest.

"That's my boy! That's my boy a hundred times over," says the father, forgetting himself in his joy and throwing the little boy up into the air, as if he were a ball.

That baby became Paramasivam, and with the consciousness of the differences between I, you and he, began to learn those games which are handed down from one generation to another. Gradually, the list of things he was acquainted with, grew – Appa, Amma, the street, the town. Then the Teacher, his cane, some schooling, trivial bits of learning, and in spite of the cane, there were some bits of wisdom, sweet, necessary and loved which Paramasivam came to acquire, and from different market places, too. Several notions such as sugar is sweet, fire burns, father will be angry, God will not forgive – some learnt from direct experience, some without any experience whatsoever – began to raise walls about him, and build a house whose foundation was "I" and "Mine." And a generous time structure made of the days of the week allowed him to explore a number of paths such as school – Paramasivam – blow – kick – strength – and the game of balin chadugudu.

The time came for him to take on Azhagiyanambiya Pillai's professional duties. Paramasivam became Paramasivam Pillai. His body grew in proportion and beauty. He gained strength in his muscles, firmness in mind, courage and hope in his heart. There came a virtuous woman who cooked for him, and assisted him to carry on the family lineage. What happiness in the heightening of breath and its release! What acute pleasure! All the strength of his body flooded, scattering life-seeds.

And now, how to describe the hastening of days, weeks and months? Difficulties, bitterness, disappointment. Was it five years already, since he took that loan? How fast it all goes. What can run so fast as the last of the sand, when the sand-cage sinks? Can it be true that Mondays and Tuesdays have never gone so fast as they do now? ... Or is it I who am running? ... Who am I? This body? Where is this I when I sleep? Where was it before I was born? Is it this I who is running? Is it I who run? Endless accounts at the desk. Back breaking work. From bending down to support another's money bags, I have even sprained my neck. My back is hunched, now. In quest of another man's good, scraping a few coins together, my eyes can only see at a distance. At home the cat's asleep. There is a climate of lies. Poverty takes my own child by the hand, and plays in a circle. The beauty that shone from my wife's eyes – that beauty that so much provoked and seduced the beholder – where has it gone? Why are my hands so empty? As for the fields, they are mortgaged. And as for the house, it is positively doing yogic exercises in order to return to primal Nature. Once the crossbeam falls down, the house will be no more ... Then where will Azhagiyanambiya Pillai be? Where will his son Paramasivam be? Everything will be obliterated in the eternal flow. How many anxieties! And how many disappointments following upon how many hopes! One god to grant good taste to the mouth. Another god to irrigate the fields. For victory in litigation. For the astrological prediction to come out right. And then, a god to worship truly, with faith and devotion for many days. How many, how many. Did all these gods appear, after my birth, and for my sake alone? And if there are so many for my sake, how many would there be in all, for all those endless body-minds in the river of life? One can, perhaps, count the grains of sand on the shores of the river. But these gods? If one man is born, how many gods are born with him? And will they die along with him? Does the "I" die? In that case, they too might die along with this "I." Yet there must be gods who remain, despite the "I." These are the fine rootlets that attempt to stabilize that something called the "Mind," which plays with mud houses, on the shores of Time's flood ... Paramasivam, Paramasivam! Why do you trouble yourself with these thoughts, da? There, just at your feet, there is a snake, da, a snake!

Rope serpent. Illusion.

Time, a rope serpent?

They moved Paramasivam from his bed and laid him on the floor. How is it possible to survive a snakebite? Someone sat by his bed, chanting a tevaram in order that the departing soul might be blessed. Paramasivam looked up and spoke with difficulty, "It would be more comforting if you could chant from a distance, please ... If you are too close, it bothers me, like a bee buzzing in my ear."

He felt a certain happiness in looking at the world partially, through eyes that were neither closed nor open. The tevaram, chanted at a distance, was as comforting as the sound of humming from afar, as he sat under water ... There, I can see my book! ... Yes, that's my big toe. For how long will I be able to see it? But I don't seem to be conscious of my feet! Is it enough just to see it? Should I not be conscious of feeling it, too? But my toe is at a

Pudumaippittan

great distance from me. At least two miles away. Chi, it must be at least eight miles off. There's my book. It looks as if it is very far away, too. What did I write in it? Accounts? Or verses? I must call Azhigiyanambi and ask him. But what does it matter, what it is? When I die, this big toe will turn into ashes. I wonder for how long I will be able to look at it. Suppose I just do so, for a while, peacefully. Yes, that feels good, too. Do I feel sleepy? Do I feel a great weariness coming over me? What if I were to shut my eyes quietly. Appa, what peace ... Breath stops. Thumbs draw inwards. Organs cease to function. The "I" spins. Consciousness swirls. Life, yes, life departs. That piece of flesh which stayed within the womb, formless, so long ago, lies withered today, fully formed.

The ashes have scattered with the wind. The name has disappeared among names. The human mind built a million million similar cages, and played amongst them. The marudam tree in Kailasapuram gave its shade. The trees flowered, fruited, ripened. The river waters tumbled over the sand and the stone steps. Does it matter, whether it is Kallipatti or Kailasapuram? The floods of time keep on flowing past, never stagnant. In it there are no limits nor bounds. You cannot see any lines. Is this the city of the womb or is it the last cremation ground? Is this moment the final samadhi or the beginning of consciousness? Does it matter which it is?

If I move, Time moves. If I cease, Time ceases. Does Time move? Sunday, Monday, Tuesday. Time lasts as long as I last. If that "I" ceases, then Time ends. Time is an illusion, a rope serpent.

Where is Paramasivam Pillai?

translation or adaptation

some friends and i were exchanging pleasantries the other day. The conversation took a leap from China to Lord Siva, jumped from there to Pure Tamil, and finally sought sanctuary in the *Ananda Vikatan* Deepavali issue.

"Have you seen our special issue?" asked a friend.

"No, I haven't," I replied.

"It seems Sri Swaminathan too has contributed something," put in another friend.

"It's an adaptation, but he has done it quite well," said the first friend.

The original article first appeared in *Manikkodi* in November 1937. This translation is from *Annai Itta Thi,* Kalachchuvadu Pathippagam, Nagercoil, 1998 .

I said, "This commerce in adaptation is altogether a terrible thing. If even reputable writers who ought to know a thing or two go in for this business, then it seems very much as if they are validating those editors who are forever seeking the favour of the general public, just to fill their bellies."

Having stepped outside to spit out a mouthful of betel juice, another friend said, "For some reason you seem to expect a great deal from Sri Swaminathan. When has he ever written a story entirely by himself?"

At this, the gentleman who introduced the journal in the first place, cut in, "What you say is altogether wrong. Adaptation ought certainly to be permitted. In fact we must do it. There is nothing at all wrong in it."

When we render a story from a foreign land into Tamil, is it best to translate it, or to adapt and rewrite it?

That is the question.

I felt a desire to develop my thoughts at greater length when the opportunity presented itself. My friend, Ka Naa Subramaniam too supported the "Adaptation" party. On a certain occasion, long ago, he had suggested that we debate the issue through our journals. I decided I would write my piece in order to learn what he too might have to say about this topic.

As a prologue to my views on the subject, I think it best to clarify a couple of terms.

Translation: To translate a story means that to the best of our ability, to the very extent that the flexibility of our language allows, we present to our readers the product of a foreign culture without jeopardizing its very essence.

Adaptation: This is to take the chief events of a narrative from a foreign land, and to elaborate upon them, more-or-less in the same way as the original, without there being any necessity to retain all its literary aspects.

Recently some people have lifted the sun and put it in their pockets, calling it adaptation. This is mere theft.

Those who contend that a story must be adapted belong to one party. Their argument is that Tamil people will never enjoy reading about foreign codes of behaviour, because they can never understand them. If this were true, of course, we need not even think about stories from foreign lands. A further branch of this argument states that the author will be hard put to find a sequence of events in Tamil culture, exactly similar to that in the original. This statement is actually a measuring rod which reveals the lack of talent amongst these people, for writing fiction. People who take this line measure themselves with their own words.

There is another faction which says, "Why sir, Shakespeare never invented a single story of his own. He too, picked up his plots from here and there and adapted them, sir. I suppose we should only praise the great ones who do it?"

If we are to allow theft today simply on the grounds that it happened in the past, then we might as well close down all our prisons. But Shakespeare did not steal as some people say he did – that is to say, he did not Adapt in the sense in which these people use the term. If he took the Hamlet story, for instance, he used the same characters openly, there was no stealth about it. It wasn't a case, as with our writers, of "Bertrand" becoming "Periyasami Nadar." In the plays, it is true, German Hamlets become English ones, but it must not be forgotten that they remain as Hamlets.

Pudumaippittan

Some learned fellows might ask, "Why sir, what about Aesop's fables? Is it necessary to translate these too?" (I am not insisting that the cats and monkeys which turn up in Aesop's fables must carry the marks of having lived during the Roman Empire. Aesop was a Greek slave of Roman times. The Romans of the period were eager to recruit Greek tutors among their slaves, just as some people today collect stamps or cigarette cards, according to the fashion. It is now thought that these stories spread from India in ancient times and that they were first created here. Hence the joke.) There can actually be no discussion about these and other stories which belong to a world literature. Like the ocean and the sky, they belong to everyone. But just as the sea and the sky appear in different lights and colours depending upon their context and climate, so these stories will sparkle in different colours at different times and places. But only an expert such as Fitzgerald can take a poem with the special form which its own culture gives it, and translate it, preserving its essential beauty. I mention Fitzgerald as an example of someone who was able to translate a text from a foreign literature, without any loss of its particular fragrance.

It was in this context that I wanted to comment on Sri Swaminathan's story. It must be apparent only to those who research into ancient history that this story originated in India. It is not at all the sort that we commonly talk about or recognize.

Sri Swaminathan is often praised as one who has learnt a foreign language with some imagination, and who has the ability to impart it to others without loss of its special quality. This particular story appears to have been taken from Chaucer, who is renowned in English Literature as the forefather of storytellers.

Not only has Sri Swaminathan lost a rare opportunity to give the Tamil reader some idea of Chaucer's skill in storytelling, he has validated with an absolute seal of approval, those who go about stealing copyright in the name of adaptation. Whether this was an error that was made in ignorance, or a wrong committed in full knowledge, at least let it be rectified from now on. That will be enough.

What is one's particular aim when telling a story from a different land? The translator engages in the same task as the author of historical novels. Such an author moves about in time. So does the translator. (I am speaking of the translation of contemporary stories.) This is the difference. The writer of historical novels takes ancient people who have been nothing more than cold copper plates and fallen victory towers, gives them flesh, blood and feelings, and makes them converse with us. The translator is exactly alike in intention. He attempts to reveal the living, throbbing human nature which lies behind what may appear to be a strange and unusual language and dress.

It is my belief that there is no justice at all in the commerce known as adaptation.

to kamala: extract from a letter to his wife

when i said you should take comfort in your faith in God, I was asking you to harness the gifts that are yours by nature, which are part of your own inmost character. At times I have watched you from my own position of disbelief, and have even envied you. As for me, I continue to think that there is nothing at all that I can bow to in worship, there is only perpetual nothingness. What is bhakti? It is only the belief that we have shifted all our heart's troubles on to something unknown, and the strength that comes from this belief. Who knows whether there really is something outside ourselves which will bear all our burdens? We are comforted, anyway, if only we can stand

The original extract was first published in *Kanmani Kamalavukku*, ed. Ilayabharati, Santhi Prasuram, Chennai, 1994.

within that belief, without examining it too carefully.

I'll tell you another thing. It is true, we don't have to go out of our way to welcome adversities. But when they do come to us, we should never try to run away. And after all, we cannot ever run away from them, really. The struggle to escape only increases our suffering. No, the only way to overcome our troubles is to stand firm against them. I'll give you an example of how we might achieve that strength. Say we have gone to bathe at the seaside. Wave upon wave is coming towards us. Now, it's certain that anyone who sees a huge breaker hurrying towards him and tries to run away from it will only be thrown face down to the ground, his eyes and nose filling with sand and salt water. But if we are brave enough, we could face that wave and leap above it. Or else we could bow before it, plunge right into it, and let it roll over us. Until it has washed across our backs, we can have no other course but to submit to it as if we have been completely overcome. Once it has gone, though? But if we are afraid of that, if we can just gather enough courage, we can face that wave, leap right up and make good our escape with not even a drop of water on our faces. Our lives in this world are full of experiences like this.

Kannamma, I've used whatever skill I have to put together a makeshift philosophy that can be of comfort to you. But, Kannamma, you know that I cannot even bear to think of you being there, alone and so far away from me.

Pudumaippittan

on rabindranath tagore

it has to be said that great as Tagore's
poems are, his short stories are even greater. Each one of them,
one could say, is a prose-poem in itself. Not only do these stories
go to the very heart of a human being, they also create an entire
world of their own. Then, one could write a whole Bharatam on
the complex structure of the stories. It could be that it is the author
alone who must understand best the fine points of artistry and
form of the stories he writes. The result though, is truly a feast
for the receptive reader.

There is a proverb that says that it takes the serpent's tail to

The original review of the two volumes, *Short Stories by Tagore,* translated by
Bharatiyaar and V V S Aiyer and *Short Stories by Tagore*, translated by Sri Sri
Achaaryaar, was first published in *Manikkodi* in October 1936. This translation
is from *Annai Itta Thi*, Kalachchuvadu Pathippagam, Nagercoil, 1998.

know the serpent. One of the translators of these stories is himself a poet. Another is an accomplished critic. In other words, he is one who has an insider's understanding of how a poem works, he is a mute poet. The third can be described as the most sensitive and perceptive of readers. All three have translated from the source language, Bengali.

All three translators were participants in the Tamil renaissance, at its very daybreak. Bharatiyaar has translated four stories for the first book, while V V S Aiyer has translated one. Sri Sri Acharyaar has translated five stories for the second book.

Anyone who is looking for excellent stories in Tamil – and there are few enough of these – ought certainly to buy both these books.

on the bachelor of arts by r k narayan

all tamil people can take pride in what Sri R K Narayan has achieved. He has written a novel in English, called *The Bachelor of Arts*, which has been much acclaimed in England. However, it is to be regretted that an author who has been praised highly by renowned writers and critics such as E M Forster should remain a foreigner in his own land, Tamil Nadu. I admit that it is a great skill to be able to use a foreign language with complete ease. But it can be no more than an acquired dexterity, rather like a circus feat. The thoughts which are closest to the life and being of a people can only be expressed in the language that is closest to their hearts.

The original review was first published in *Manikkodi* in August 1937. This translation is from *Annai Itta Thi*, Kalachchuvadu Pathippagam, Nagercoil, 1998.

That alone becomes literature. However fine a testimony *The Bachelor of Arts* might be to Sri Narayan's skill, the story it tells will remain counterfeit. That is to say, Sri Narayan's attempt has only been to look at our country through English eyes. I have digressed so far from my usual path for one reason alone – the hope that Sri Narayan will introduce himself to the Tamil people he writes about, at least now.

An English translation of the Bengali poet Rabindranath Tagore's poems has been reviewed in the Christmas issue of the British Literary journal, *London Mercury*. People who read it will find that it illustrates my point quite clearly. The critic explains with great emphasis, for the length of two columns, how wrong he has been in his reading of Bengali poems thus far, and ends at last by commending the Bengali poet for his ability to write in English. If this is to be the fate of a great poet who creates indestructible dreams in his own language, one can only wonder what will happen to everyone else. Writers who receive worldwide or international fame ought to find a place in the minds and hearts of their own people, first of all.

about tamil

about the tamil language – but
here, some might attack me for not using the term, Pure Tamil.
Well, let those who wish to place their mother on the funeral pyre
and then rejoice write what they like. About the Tamil language
then, a unique lament over loss of faith is being raised these days.
There is a certain confusion here. Some say that Tamil was once
a renowned language. (Though not for its literature.) They fear
that this proud reputation is now being lost. They fear that the
Celestial Damsel, Tamil, might marry outside her community.
Hence the attempt to hide her behind the screen of Isolation,
and turn her into a pure maiden, protected by Dogma against
the arrows of Dissent.

The original article was first published in *Gandhi* in June 1934. This translation
is from *Annai Itta Thi*, Kalachchuvadu Pathippagam, Nagercoil, 1998.

Language is a powerful weapon. It can both reveal the inner mind and conceal it. If it is left in its scabbard unused, it will rust. This could be the fate of our language too.

For some time we have been behaving in a manner that is quite contrary to nature. Language is the life-force of a society. It is in our own language that we can speak of our innermost feelings most powerfully. It is because we forgot about this fact of nature that our own language has become foreign to us. Not knowing now, where to begin the remedy, we hang on to the raft of Sangam, only to flounder and capsize.

Language is a flourishing karpagavalli, a fabled golden creeper, watered and nourished by Time. At this present moment of renewed power, of a Tamil Renaissance, to make garlands of verses from fallen and withered leaves and to call that linguistic progress is fitting only for camels who can have no sense of beauty.

Tamil is not an insolvent language. The addition of new words is not going to destroy her individuality. She is a queen. For her to receive new words is the same as conquering new countries and reaching towards storehouses full of new cultural treasures. This is the subtle secret of the nature of language. Kamban knew this well. The writers and artists who were his contemporaries knew it too. In Kamban's poetry, new words – resonating, mouth-filling Sanskrit words – are like ornaments to the Goddess of Beauty.

Prose

Until the present time, Tamil prose has had no real standing. There are three reasons for this. The first is common to all societies. Early man was aware only of grand and uncontrollable emotions. These were all he knew and all he experienced. Starting from movement and ecstatic dance, these came to completion in dance-drama. And beginning with song – mere shouts and chants at first – they took shape as poetry. He began to store these away. These are our earliest literatures. This is the secret why all early literatures exist in the form of songs.

The reason for Tamil prose having remained at the level of speech until the present is that we have used palm leaves as our main means of preserving our literature. It is impossible to write a long prose-epic on palm leaves. Because of this alone, prose was given the name Urainadai or speech-style. And ever since prose (as that which gives meaning to song) became the hand maiden of the Goddess of Poetry, the learned poets began to consider it shameful even to speak in prose. So everything, starting from a letter to a patron was turned into rhyming and mechanical verse. And prose, in Tamil, remained an undeveloped tool.

If we are to give prose the status that it deserves, then we must put away our rusted modes of thinking. It is a huge mistake to think that a distance ought to be maintained between literary Tamil and spoken Tamil. If that situation should continue, there is no doubt at all that slowly and gradually, Tamil will die. Between literary Tamil and spoken Tamil there is only one difference. Literary Tamil is the handiwork of the creative writer, polished by his aesthetic sense. Spoken Tamil is the uncut diamond which reflects the very heartbeat just as it is. It is spoken Tamil that is the life-force, the creative writer's storehouse. If we raise a wall between these two, Tamil's fate will be the very same as that of Greek, Latin and Sanskrit.

A sentence has a life of its own. It is a creation with muscles and nerves and organs. We should never think of it as a mere word chain made up of compound nouns. The architectonics of a sentence is extremely important. The arrangements of words within a sentence can yield fine distinctions of meanings. There is a music in sentences and their rhythm, in prose as in poetry. Yet it is more subtle. It comes out of the artistry of the words and the beauty of the sentence structure. It is impossible to explain how this comes about. It is acquired through practice alone, by reading the works of the great writers over and over again, and through experience. Nor are there many role models whom we can follow in Tamil. We need to look for them elsewhere. Some people seem to think that the music of prose lies in the liberal use of alliteration and internal rhyme. For me, this only brings to mind the story told by Kamban, of the asuna bird which was so engrossed by certain notes of music that a sudden and loud beat of drums caused it to die instantly. To write in such a bombastic way is obscene, to speak in that fashion is madness.

Words are the living atoms which transport the life-force of a language. Rather than excavate and string together words which were once in use, but now lie rusting in the dictionaries, one might fondle a coconut seedling which has been buried deep, pretending it is a real child. It was in the full knowledge of the secret of words that our ancient artists celebrated our language as Payant-Tamil or Pasunt-Tamil, that is, a powerful and living spoken Tamil. This is the very meaning of the words which Avvai, foremother of Tamil literature, used when she wanted to describe the special quality of Tamil, "The beauty of familiar words." It is only if we wish to lose the ideal of the beauty of the familiar and choose instead the beauty of the dead, that we should apply ourselves to digging mines in the dictionary.

In order to write in a prose style which appeals to one's sense of beauty, one needs a knowledge of several languages, and the ability to learn from their best attributes. In this matter, the pundits cannot help us. We cannot expect from them either artistic sensibility or creative force. Both these are like cargos which the sea has swallowed up, as it once swallowed up the city of Kabadapuram.

As for the new pundits who are riding the crest of the recent flood of popularity of English, they quite outdo the old pundits. These fakes, with their absurd style and opinions should be put to one side like counterfeit coins. And if Tamil – currently imprisoned by both these sets of pundits – is to be set free, how is it to be done by universities which are supposed to be institutions which foster art and which are engaged instead in picking up any monstrous text in Tamil even before the ink on it is dry, and passing it off as a textbook?

That leaves the journals. Not those that claim to be written in the service of Pure Tamil prose, but those which are published on the understanding that what is written is meant to be read. It is such journals that must take on this huge responsibility. It may be that they cannot of themselves, create literature, but they can certainly accustom their readers to a flexible prose style.

making it new: pudumaippittan and the tamil short story, 1934-48

pudumaippittan is the pen name of Cho Vrittasalam, who, along with Mauni and other contributors to the seminal journal, *Manikkodi,* transformed the short story and naturalized it into the Tamil language in the second half of the 1930s, self-consciously "Making it new." The pen name Cho Vrittasalam chose for himself means "Crazy for the new," "Fervent for" or "Possessed by the new," and has led to endless play by critics on the two elements that form it. At the end of an essay entitled "My stories and I," Pudumaippittan quotes from a critic who had said of his work, that you could largely see in it pittam, "Madness," with here and there some pudumai, "Newness." With superb self-confidence, Pudumaippittan agrees with the critic. He refers to a famous line from a Tamil Tevaram which addresses Siva himself as Pittan, "Pitta, piraicudi, perumaane" (Madman, crescent-wearer, my Lord). Pudumaippittan comments, "I will assume that this critic is referring to the frenzied paradoxes contained in that image (of Siva as Nataraaja), and accept all those for myself too ... what is new in my work is the substance I give to that (creative) frenzy."[1]

Pudumaippittan came from a Saiva vellala family, and was born in 1906, in Thiruppathirippuliyur where his father was known as Tahsildar Chokkalingam Pillai. He left home with his wife soon after he took his BA degree, having quarrelled with his father. From this time on, he worked on a series of newspapers, first on the *Oozhiyan*, a Reformist journal inspired by the Self Respect Movement and edited by Raya Chokkalingam in Karaikkudi, then in Chennai on the *Dinamani,* and yet later on the *Dinasari.* He was an extremely prolific writer. Besides about a hundred short stories, published in *Kalaimagal, Manikkodi,* and other journals, he also wrote one-act plays, a few poems, (which he published under the name Velur Ve Kandaswamy Kaviraayar), and a number of translations and adaptations as well as book reviews and critical articles. He instigated and participated in some of the famous literary debates of the time, (for example about the value of translation as against adaptation), in most of which Kalki Krishnamurti was his chief target and antagonist. In his last few years, he left his newspaper commitments hoping to start an independent literary journal, *Sodanai,* which never came off, and also began writing film scripts. He was in Pune, putting the finishing touches to the film script, *Rajamukti,* when it was diagnosed that both his lungs were damaged by tuberculosis. He died in Tiruvananthapuram a few months later, in 1948. He was only forty two years old.

Pudumai, newness, when applied to his work has a range of meanings that I explore in this essay. It refers to his consciousness of using a new genre, the short story, his deliberate experimentation in forms and styles, and his awareness of taking the new Tamil Literature into the modern literary world. But it also refers to the freshness of perspective in his use of this genre, particularly in his observation of Tamil Nadu during the fourteen years of his writing career, the beliefs and practices, the social change and the shifting political affiliations that he saw about him. His contemporary and equally important Tamil writer Mauni, who outlived him by three decades, said that the overwhelming tone of Pudumaippittan's work is irony. In an era of Gandhian idealism, perhaps it was Pudumaippittan's cool ironic gaze – despite his own undoubted social commitment – that was seen to be so strikingly new by his contemporaries.

Pudumaippittan wrote three essays on the development of the short story in Tamil. First of all, he distinguishes Story or narrative material from Short Story as literary genre. He also distinguishes between the novel, a mirror reflecting the world, and the short story, a window which affords a framed perspective upon it. Looking back over fifty years, he takes Selvakesavaraya Mudaliar (1864-1921) and his *Abinava Kadaigal* as his starting point, and marks three stages. The first, from Selvakesavaraya Mudaliar to V V S Aiyar, he describes as a trial period. The next stage, is the period of V V S Aiyar who, Pudumaippittan claims, gave life and form to the short story, particularly in his collection *Mangayarkkarasi's Love and Other Stories* (1917). The third stage, he says, is the impetus given to the short story in the 1930s with the proliferation of journals and magazines, the rise of a certain kind of popular comic tale told for laughs (by Kalki in particular), and a great wave of translation and adaptation from fiction in other Indian languages as well as English. And then, the journal *Manikkodi* appeared in 1933.

Manikkodi began as a largely political weekly under the editorship of V Ramaswamy and T S Chokkalingam. The name, meaning Jewelled banner, is from a nationalist poem by Subramanya Bharati. A year later, B S Ramaiah and V Ramaswamy were editing it under a new format, and it had become a fortnightly literary magazine carrying several short stories, literary criticism, book reviews and short fiction in translation. By 1936 some of the most important writers of the time were contributing to it. Pudumaippittan says that in the hands of such writers as Ku Pa Rajagopalan, Picchamurti, B S Ramaiah, Shanmugasundaram, Mauni and himself, the Tamil short story finally came into its own. In his words,

[We were] able to construct and reveal in words, life's several subtleties. Short fiction which had revelled in moonlight, love, hero and heroine cast away the belief that Siva himself would suddenly appear and grant a boon, and that the sorrows suffered by a pativrata [devoted wife] must inevitably cease, and began instead to look steadily at life, at the truth.[2]

It is this realism, Pudumaippittan says, combined with literary skill, that was new in the *Manikkodi* contribution to the development of the Tamil short story.

Man's humiliations, his mistakes, his attempts to overcome them – it took a long time to re-create this as literature, to write about these things with creative skill. Just as one was beginning to think that there was no hope at all for Tamil, a few new writers appeared, welcome as the morning star.[3]

Pudumaippittan's word for realism is Yadaartam. The word comes into Tamil critical terminology with him, modern critics use yadaartavaadam. Not all Pudumaippittan's fiction is in the realistic mode, he was also interested in the psychology of fantasy, dream and myth as modes of fictionalizing. But he was deeply interested in exploring the limits of realism, and what he could do with it. Thus, the new realism becomes a tool, in his earliest stories, to satirise mercilessly those kinds of Newness that he rejects, the superficial Westernization of certain groups (for example, the brown sahibs, or durais on the tea plantations) and above all, the dehumanizing urbanization that he sees around him in the Chennai city of his day.

The nagaram, City, becomes a symbol, in many of his stories, of a mechanical Modern culture. There are repeated references in the early (1934 -1938) short, stark and shocking stories to the hurrying crowds, the increased traffic, the incessant noise of the trams. "Mahamasaanam" (The Great Cremation Ground, 1941) begins, When evening falls, the city changes, as if it wants to prove that civilization is just a highway on which you can move forward only by jostling others and being jostled yourself, in return.[4]

The title of the story is the Tamilized form of the Sanskrit maha smasaana, which actually refers to Banaras as the ultimate cremation ground. Pudumaippittan's "Mahamasaanam" consists of just one scene at the Roundtana in Mount Road in Madras. An old Muslim beggar lies there, dying, attended by a younger man. They are watched by a small girl who sees it all as a piece of entertainment during the short period of time when her father crosses the road to buy mangoes. The shocking incident is baldly told. The story ends as the child is carried away by her father, her attention only upon the mango in her hand. Nobody at all has noticed anything unusual, of death happening in the midst of life. The story encapsulates an entire way of life, both by its images, the details it focuses upon, and by the starkness of the author/spectator's perspective and style.

If "Mahamasaanam" is placed in one of the Nerve centres of the city, "Ponnagaram" (The Golden City) and "Kavundanum Kaamanum" (Hunger and Love), both of 1934, are set in the city's slums, a maze of narrow lanes and open gutters where children play, crammed with cage-like dwellings without electric lights and adequate water supply, where the new mill workers are packed. Both these stories are centred around incidents in which young women in the slums have to take to prostitution in order to eke out a living, they contain some of Pudumaippittan's darkest indictment of modern city life.

In his later work, particularly in the fiction published in a 1943 collection, there is a different emphasis in the City stories. These come closest to his own description of the new realism which I quoted earlier, "To write with creative skill about man's humiliations, his mistakes, his attempts to overcome them." Several of these, such as "Chellammal," "Subbayya Pillaiyin Kaadalgal" (The Affairs of Subbayya Pillai), "Kadavulum Kandasami Pillaiyum" (God and Kandasami Pillai) and "Manida Yandiram" (The Human Machine) are stories of displacement from village into town, and alienation there.

Pudumaippittan writes repeatedly of a lower middle class Pillai (a member of the Saiva vellala farming or landowning caste, Pudumaippittan's own community) typically also from a village in Tirunelveli district, who has left the joint family for one reason or another, and come to Chennai with his wife, and who ekes out a living, most often by working all hours in a shop, owned by another Pillai. In "Chellammal," the relations between the Manager Pillaivaal and Brahmanayagam Pillai who works for him are described succinctly, caste loyalties are harnessed in new ways to commercial ends in a new urban scenario, the older and richer man exploits the younger, but he is also the benefactor and protector. Pudumaippittan writes with great insight into the day-to-day economic struggle in families of this sort the repetition of daily routine, the tragedy of isolation.

In all these City stories, even in the bleakest of them such as "Mahamasaanam," or "Chellammal," what emerges is the survival of human dignity and worth as Pudumaipittan sees it, in spite of the faceless and monstrous urban culture that seeks to oppress it. It is significant that "Mahamasaanam" ends with a kind of affirmation, the little girl turns away from the spectacle of death to smell the mango in her hand. But it must be emphasized that it is almost always the bleak survival of the human being that he presents, alone, without societal or supernatural supports.

In contrast to these stories about the new urbanization, Pudumaippittan wrote a number of stories which are set in the very villages that the pillais in exile idealize. Here Pudumaippittan takes an opposite stance, seeing them rather as entrenched in their social hierarchy, resisting new ideas, slow to change. Many of these villages are remote, too insignificant even to be shown on the district map. Although he does describe one or two mainly brahmin agraharam villages, most of the villages in his stories are dominated by pillais. Most powerful among these is the pannaiyar pillai, who owns most of the land, leasing some of it to the other pillais, who form a tight group around him, protecting vellala interests.

In these villages of Pudumaippittan's stories, the paraiyas in the cheri (or Untouchable quarter) remain the slaves of the aandai, the landowner. Besides, they are the slaves of the invisible white masters, the durais. Whereas the upper caste brahmins and pillais can leave for the town, the only escape route available for the poor is to go to Sri Lanka as plantation labourers. In one of the best known among his early stories, "Thunbakeni" (A Well of Sorrows, 1934), Marudi and her mother, paraiya women, are driven because of their poverty to go to Sri Lanka with the kangaani, the agent sent by the tea estate to recruit Indian labour for the plantation. Unusually, the protagonist of this story is a woman. She is exploited, raped first by the store manager and then by the white plantation manager and gets the white man's disease, but survives bravely until her own daughter, Vellacchi is raped by the very same store manager. The story is written in Pudumaippittan's early stark style, and reads almost like notes for a novel. It brings out the courage and spirit of the two women, but also suggests that they cannot win, the escape routes of the poor prove to be illusory.

The resistance to change, particularly in regard to caste hierarchy, which he so much deplores, is linked to a central concern in Pudumaippittan's works – the conflict between ascriptive hierarchy and its interests, and the new egalitarianism. Pudumaippittan treats this theme in a very wide ranging way, seeing it from many angles, setting it against the political background of E V Ramaswamy Naicker's Self Respect Movement, Christian missionary activity and Gandhi's Harijan Uplift Movement, particularly Gandhi's visit to Tamil Nadu during 1933-34. A social vision of equal dignity and worth goes back in modern times in Tamil Nadu to Ramalinga Swamigal (1823-1874) and Subramanya Bharati (1882-1921), and even before them, to the Siddhar, medieval mystics of no particular caste or sect, whose songs are still popular. Ramalinga Swami inspired the Self Respecters especially, while the songs of Bharati were used by Self Respecters and Congress members alike in their marches and demonstrations.

Between 1925 and 1929, Ramaswamy Naicker was the chief architect and organizer of the Self Respect Movement, with its emphasis on rationality and its goals of removing brahmins from positions of power, eradicating untouchability, encouraging marriages between sub castes and raising the position of women. By 1929, it had become a formidable movement with several young leaders. Gandhi's Harijan Uplift Movement (which took off in the wake of his fast in protest against the proposed Communal Award which would grant separate electorates for Untouchables and others) must be seen against this background in Tamil Nadu. The Self Respecters overlapped with Congress in many of their concerns, but their increasingly strident anti religious stance was in sharp contrast to Gandhi's Harijan Uplift Movement which stayed within the framework of a (restated) Hindu dharma. Besides, the Gandhian approach was top down, using upper caste leadership, while the Self Respecters agitated for grass roots solidarity. In the 1930s the Harijan Uplift Movement in Tamil Nadu had several different thrusts - consciousness raising, the temple entry movement and breaking of caste rules, specifically in the case of inter marriage. All these themes appear both in the novels and in the short fiction of the time.

B S Ramaiah, who edited *Manikkodi* after it changed its format from a political weekly into a fortnightly dedicated to publishing short fiction, writes that the Gandhian ideal, that "Everyone should be measured alike and valued alike" became a basic assumption of the new literature of the times. He claims that all the essays of Va Ramaswamy, the previous editor, had aimed at inculcating a concern for the person in the next house, the next street, the next town. Ramaiah writes, "When I look at the first issue of *Manikkodi* in its new format, even after all these years, it is this that stands out above all its other literary aims."[5]

But "Thunbakeni" was one of the highlights of that very issue, and the whole point of that story is the failure of the egalitarian aim. Ramaiah himself tells us that the story was published in *Manikkodi* with an epigraph that reversed each line of a famous couplet of Bharati. Pudumaippittan's version said,

> We will show our contempt for those who labour
> and till the land
> We will praise those who feast and live at leisure.

(Not the words of Bharati: but the truth)

Pudumaipittan, writing a decade after Bharati died, neither shared the ringing optimism of Bharati's songs, which seemed to suggest that an egalitarian utopia was achievable, even inevitable along with freedom, nor was he overtly a Gandhian or Self Respecter. It is clear from his many unsparing descriptions of the horrific atrocities perpetrated on the untouchables that his sympathies are undoubtedly with them, but his scepticism regarding the solutions offered by the different political groups and their success is pervasive. He suggests that for the greater part neither the upper castes nor the untouchables had quite understood nor accepted Bharati's and Gandhi's messages of equality and their implications for change, the thrust of his satire is the gap between a ready emotional response and true social change. There are, he grants, a few sincerely committed workers in the cause of eradicating untouchability, but they are ineffective, the odds stacked against them are too great.

Besides this, Pudumaippittan always tends to focus on individuals rather than on general trends and movements, tending to place the maverick individual fighting for new ideas against a hostile and conservative society. So, if there are a few brahmins in his stories who are dedicated to the eradication of untouchability, there are also a few untouchables, both men and women, who are prepared against all odds to fight for their rights. Examples of both kinds appear in the emblematic story, "Pudiya Nandan" (A New Nandan, 1934).

Significantly, this story was written by Pudumaippittan during the year of Gandhi's tour of Tamil Nadu, and made specific reference to it. The story is set in Adanur, birthplace of the puranic Nandan, who, though an outcaste, was purified by fire and granted entry into the presence of Siva at Chidambaram, along with "Those who wear the sacred thread." He then became one of the sixty three canonized Saivite saints. Nandanaar's story is told in the twelfth century *Periyapuranam* of Sekizhaar, in which he is known as "Tirunaalaypovaar, The-saint-who-would-go-(to Chidambaram)-on-the-morrow." From the late nineteenth century, this story became very widely known in Gopalakrishna Bharati's dramatic version, consisting of a cycle of songs. Nandan became a powerful symbol of the possibility of an end to caste restrictions and the availability of sacred spaces to all people. Pudumaippittan's version, however, is full of irony as he takes up the story of the paraiyas and priests of Adanur, several centuries later. Karuppan, direct descendent of Nandan, now sixty, dared in his youth to drink a mouthful of water from the temple tank of the brahmin agraharam. Viswanatha Sraudi, then quite a young priest, beat Karuppan so badly that he blinded him. Taking pity on him later, he installed him as caretaker of his fields. The story actually concerns the sons of these two. Ramanathan, son of the orthodox Viswanatha Sraudi becomes a devotee of Gandhi, works for the Harijan movement, and scandalizes his father by proposing temple entry for untouchables. He also scandalizes Karuppan by offering to marry his daughter. Karuppan's son, Pavadai, on the other hand, goes through several transformations. He converts to Christianity, is disappointed by the caste structures he finds among the Christian community, and finally becomes active in the Self Respect Movement, calling himself Comrade Narasingam. Narasingam can make no headway in persuading either his father, or the Paraiya community as a whole, to break with caste rules. Neither young man's idealism succeeds in bringing about equality. The story ends with the deaths of both young men and Karuppan in a collision with the very train that they hope is bringing Gandhi to Adanur. In the event, the Madras Mail doesn't even stop at Adanur and Gandhi never appears. "Which of these was the new Nandan?" Pudumaippittan asks. He comments, "Two people saw a new light. They saw it in two different ways. Of course they were sacrifice to society. But who thinks about that?"[6]

Unlike his rather more nuanced view of the new egalitarian movements of Gandhi and Ramaswamy Naicker, and their success or lack of it, Pudumaippittan's scepticism about Christian missionary activity is unqualified, and therefore, his satire is biting when he writes about them. In the first place, in his stories, he cannot separate Christian missions from collusion with colonialism. He is suspicious of their methods of conversion, which he sees as appealing either to the volatile emotions or to the financial needs of their potential converts. Some of his sharpest satire, however, is directed against the new Indian Protestant clergy or those figures who have become pillars of the Protestant churches, very often originally from Nadar families. These, he presents, as westernized men, insensitive to the needs of the poor, and similar to the white man in their attitude towards them, "Using the Bible as a Penal Code" as he puts it in "Nyaayam" (Justice, 1938) when describing Deva Irakkam Nadar, loyal British subject and bench Magistrate. Secondly, these men claim that in Christian communities Hindu atrocities such as caste distinctions are unknown, but lose no opportunity to round on untouchables who have been foolish enough to believe them. At the core of Pudumaippittan's unease, though, is his distaste for organized religions, all of which, as he sees it, suppress individual thought. He writes in "Pudiya

Kundu" (The New Cage, 1943), "Christianity says, Believe what I say, you do not have permission to think for yourself. Hinduism says, You may think what you like, but do not cross the fence of social strictures. Which of these is the greater?"[7]

The world that Pudumaippittan sees about him is described mainly through a male perspective. The pillais in Chennai are mostly described as lonely figures, perhaps with nuclear families. Their mundane and lonely lives, shaped by a dull routine, are after all what Pudumaippittan wants to communicate to his readers. The shadowy women are mostly wives and housekeepers, counterparts of their husbands in that they too lead precarious and lonely lives – the strain on the nuclear family (or a childless couple) because of exile from the village and the sudden growth of the city is often a painful sub theme. The City stories also focus on the city's prostitutes, portraying them as victims of their circumstances, and in need of compassion rather than censure.

There are few encounters in his stories, with pudumaippen, the New woman. Pudumaippen is actually Subramanya Bharati's phrase in the first instance, meaning the ideal modern woman freed from social oppressions, ready to fight for the freedom of the country, shoulder to shoulder with her husband. The term is used rather more equivocally in the years following Bharati. Sundararajan and Sivapathasundaram point out, "When other patriots and writers, following in the path of Bharati, dreamed of this pudumaippen, they were also aware of the possible damage to our culture because of her exposure to western customs and habits, in the name of education."[8] So pudumaippen, as C S Lakshmi writes, began to feature prominently in the 1920s, in an entirely different sense, particularly in the journals addressing a readership of women, and sometimes run by women, for example *Jagan Mohini*, edited by Vai Mu Kodainayaki Ammal. In these, and in Vai Mu Ko's novels, *Vira Vasanta* and *Sudandira Paravai*, there are cautionary portraits of modern young women who are educated, fashionable, English speaking, who break caste rules and come to a bad end.[9] This kind of caricature was also persistent in *Ananda Vikatan* and other popular journals of the time.

There are only, perhaps, a couple of portraits of the modern woman in Pudumaippittan's stories, but they are strikingly different from the caricatures that C S Lakshmi mentions. They exemplify Pudumaippittan's favourite concerns of individual responsibility and freedom from social and religious restraints. There is Jaya, the Christian girl in "Pudiya Kundu," significantly, one of Pudumaippittan's few attractive portraits of Christians. In many ways, Jaya would fit in with Vai Mu Ko's blueprint of a Bad modern girl – she is Christian for a start, but she is also educated, and she falls in love with a fellow student at the Catholic college at Palayamkottai, a brahmin, Krishnamurti, or Kittu. But although her marriage to Kittu damages his family irretrievably, Jaya herself is treated sympathetically by Pudumaippittan, she comes out best of all the characters in this story because she is the one, who in the end is least constrained by rules of religion.

There is another modern girl, who makes a fleeting but impressive appearance in "Subbayya Pillaiyin Kaadalgal" (The Affairs of Subbayya Pillai, 1943). Subbayya Pillai is yet another pillai from Tirunelveli, maintaining an old fashioned, tightly regulated lifestyle in Chennai, travelling from Tambaram to

Beach station and back every day on the new electric train. He only dreams briefly of flying away somewhere, every time the train stops for two minutes at the Minambakkam station. (Minambakkam was where the new civilian airport was proposed.) In the story, a young woman boards the train at Mambalam, pushing her way ahead of the crowds, to sit in front of him. She is a medical student, she is wearing a stethoscope and carrying books, completely at ease with herself and her surroundings. Sometime before Kodambakkam, she leaves the train unnoticed, Subbayya Pillai is dreaming of freedom and romance. The huge distance between her life and his is only suggested, as are the possible choices available to each. This is one of Pudumaippittan's City stories that actually gives place to and affirms the multiplicity of individual lives and lifestyles, of both men and women, in the new Chennai that Pudumaippittan sees emerging.

Among Pudumaippitan's work, there is also a crucial story, "Sabavimochanam" (Deliverance from the Curse, 1943), which deals with women's agency. A reworking of the Ahalya story, "Sabavimochanam" begins with the release of Ahalya from her curse when Rama touches her with his foot, and she is no longer a stone statue. In the Pudumaippittan version, a very young Rama absolves Ahalya, saying that a deed has to be judged by its intention or lack of it, Ahalya cannot be held responsible for Indra's deceit to which she did not willingly consent. Many years later, Ahalya is outraged when she hears that the same Rama, aware of Sita's innocence, put her through the fire-test in order to establish the fact of her innocence publicly. As the radiant god-child, Rama can see with clarity that each deed must be judged by the individual doer's intention. Yet later, as the Ideal ruler trained by Vasishta, he puts the state and public interest first. Here Pudumaippittan is raising the whole question of the basis of moral action (dharma) and therefore of moral judgments, particularly in regard to women, and placing individual responsibility and accountability above established rules and practices. The story illuminates, in a very particular way, the Newness in Pudumaippittan's work.

Pudumaippittan said, in "En Kadaigalum Naanum" (My Stories and I), that at the core of all his stories there is a certain nambikkai varatchi, literally a drying up of belief or hope. Nambikkai varatchi is often taken to mean lack of hope or a profound pessimism. Yet, if Pudumaippittan is pessimistic about social change, he also celebrates and affirms the individual lives of those who seek change. Nambikkai varatchi, though, can also mean scepticism or agnosticism, a this-worldly and questioning position in his exploration of myths, beliefs and practices. It is to this latter sense that I now turn.

Pudumaippittan wrote a long polemical essay, "Ungal Kadai" (Your Story), which brings together many of the ideas which are reflected in his stories consistently. First of all, he presents the history of man as a constant struggle for survival. According to him, it is because of this struggle for survival that human societies grew, governments and religions developed later, as ways of safeguarding such societies. Crucially, he sees an irreconcilable contradiction between the individual and society – the individual is always sacrificed for the sake of society. Hence, he declares, his lack of faith in most political philosophers and their systems, because the ideal societies they have imagined have not taken into account the individual and his or her weaknesses. "So long as man is man, society and the individual must stand in two different corners, debating their position."[10] His suspicion of organized religion is similar. "Governments seek to fetter man's body," he writes, "Religions seek to fetter man's mind."[11] In both cases, "To be enslaved by a doctrine, kolgai, is to be enslaved by the monstrously huge forms which we have raised in the sacrificial fires we ourselves have lit."[12] The central irony for Pudumaippittan is that societies created their gods and their notions of heaven and hell according to their own needs, but then became enslaved by them. It is only by destroying the gods of our own making that we can prepare the way for genuine change.

What is new in Pudumaippittan is not simply his agnostic or questioning position, but the subtlety with which he expresses it in a variety of ways. He himself was inclined to non-belief, and was deeply suspicious of religious conversion. In view of his dislike of organized religions, he specially valued the eclecticism of modern Hinduism (which he warned, characteristically, might end by being its death-knell). He was inspired by the sheer creative energy of such Hindu symbols as the Siva Nataraaja which at different times he described as "Man's grasp of the creative principle" and "The secret of creation expressed through art." He was steeped in Saivite traditions, but resisted being Enslaved by them. Many of his last stories voice these conflicts and tensions.

Such tensions are exemplified most beautifully in "Kayittraravu," literally "Rope Serpent," or that illusory state where the rope is mistaken for a serpent. It was written in 1948, the year that Pudumaippittan died. The story is simply a stream of consciousness sequence. The protagonist, Paramasivan Pillai, squatting in the palmyra grove, reflects on the flow of time and tradition. He thinks of civilizations as toy houses made of mud on the river bank, the individual as a brief and fleeting presence. He reflects on his fifty years of life and wonders what will be left when he dies, taking away his gods with him. Yes, there will be some gods left, he thinks, the mind and its ideas, which will attempt to strengthen the mud hut on the river bank. And it is then that the snake bites him. The story ends with Paramasivam's (or Pudumaippittan's) last words, "If I move, Time moves. If I am not, Time will not be, either ... When I end, Time will end. Time is an illusion."[13]

The story suggests that individual lives are but fleeting presences in the flow of time, but all the same, individual time and its duration is all one knows. The problem is presented as a universal one, but it is also stated in Saivite terms, where Siva is Mahakala, in whose large time cycle Paramasivam's life is subsumed. But then, we are also expected to note as readers that the protagonist's name is Paramasivam, the supreme Siva, and that the town he comes from is Kailasapuram. So there is the suggestion that Paramasivan's time is collapsed into Siva's time, the only yuga one can know is one's own.

It is this complex view of tradition and belief, many layered, open ended, but on the whole sceptical and agnostic, that is new and refreshing in these last stories. They are very much more tentative and questioning than the strongly stated earlier ones such as "Ponnagaram" and other 1934 stories with their shocking view of the world. A comparison between the early and the late stories also shows the extent to which Pudumaippittan changed and developed the Tamil short story in something like fourteen years.

The contemporary novelist and critic Sundara Ramaswamy has said in an article on Pudumaippitan, "To sum up his achievement in a single sentence, he was the one who linked Tamil Literature to modern times."[14] What does this mean? Although Pudumaipittan said he was not writing just for art's sake, he was very conscious of writing in a new genre. He consciously experimented with new forms and styles. I have mentioned the stark cityscapes (for which he invented a staccato style, single sentences spread across the page, "Like a frog leaping"), and the realistic focus on ordinary lives in the cities and villages, other stories retell myths, or invent historical stories set in ancient Sangam or medieval Chola times, or use the format of a fable, or fantasy or nightmare. Sometimes he successfully mixes realism and fantasy as in "Kadavulum Kandasami Pillaiyum" (God and Kandasami Pillai), long before magic realism was invented.

He acknowledged his debt to English for teaching him about the short story, and critical approaches to this new genre. He read very widely in Tamil and in English. Ka Naa Subramaniam, who was his contemporary and wrote the introduction to the collected short stories published by Ainthinai Padippagam in 1988, lists a very wide range of contemporary fiction, both English and American, as well as in translation from French, Russian and German that Pudumaippittan read and discussed at various times with him. Yet Pudumaippittan was in no doubt at all that "It is in one's own language that one's innermost thoughts can be most powerfully expressed." He wrote this in *Manikkodi* in 1939, the year when R K Narayan's *The Bachelor of Arts* came out in England to critical acclaim. According to Pudumaippittan, such a novel, written in English could not but help look at Tamil life through Western eyes. Yet he was not chauvinistic about Tamil. As early as 1934, in an article, "Tamilai Pattri" (About Tamil) published in the journal, *Gandhi*, he dissociated himself from the Tanitttamil (pure Tamil) movement which sought to restore to Tamil its pristine purity, by getting rid of Sanskritic elements and returning to Sangam Tamil poetry as an ideal. "A language must grow according to its needs," wrote Pudumaippittan, "Adding new words as it must."[15] The way forward for Tamil was not by reviving old words from the dictionaries, but by breaking down the wall between the literary and the spoken language. He said, "Spoken language is the uncut diamond which reflects the very heartbeat just as it is (appadiappadiye)."[16] He looked neither to the pundits nor to the universities for help in achieving this, but rather to magazines and journals which know that what is written is meant to be read. Journals in themselves cannot create literature, but they can and should accustom their readers to a more flexible prose style.

Pudumaippittan knew that he belonged to an important moment in Tamil literary history. With striking self-confidence he claimed that a handful of new writers were producing short fiction in Tamil in the 1930s and 40s, which were second to none. In this select group he named B S Ramaiah, Ku Pa Rajagopalan and Mauni. He did not hesitate to include himself.

References

1. Pudumaippittan, *Pudumaippittan Kattll;'aigal* (Madras: Star Publications, 1954) 9.
2. Ibid
3. Pudumaippittan, *Pudumaippittan Katturaigal* (Madras: Star Publications, 1954) 41-2.
4. Pudumaippittan, *Pudumaippittan Padaippugal* (Collected works of Pudumaippittan) (Madras: Ainthinai Pathippagam, 1988) 58.
5. Ramaiah, B S, *Manikkodi Kalam* (Madras: Manivacagar Nulagam, 1980) 186.
6. Pudumaippittan, *Pudumaippittan Padaippttgal* (Collected works of Pudumaippittan) (Madras: Ainthinai Pathippagam, 1988) 799.
7. Pudumaippittan, *Pudumaippittan Padaippugal* (Collected works of Pudumaippittan) (Madras: Ainthinai Pathippagam, 1988) 49.
8. Sundararajan, P G & Sivapathasundaram, S, *Tamil Naaval, Nutraandu Varalaarum Valarcchiyttm* (Madras: Christian Literature Society, 1977) 135.
9. Lakshmi, C S, *The Face Behind the Mask* (New Delhi: Vikas, 1984) 104-11.
10. Pudumaippittan, *Pudumnaippittan Katturaigal* (Madras: Star Publications, 1954) 17.
11. Pudumaippittan, *Pudumaippittan Katturaigal* (Madras: Star Publications, 1954) 18.
12. Pudumaippittan, Kanmani *Kamalavttkku* (Madras: Shanti Press, 1994) 72.
13. Pudumaippittan, *Pudumaippittan Padaippugal* (Collected works of Pudumaippittan) (Madras: Ainthinai Pathippagam, 1988) 920.
14. Sundara Ramaswamy, "Tamizhukku Naviina Paarvai Tandavar" in *Dinamani* (30 June 1998).
15. Pudumaipittan, *Annai Itta Thi.* (Uncollected and Unpublished Writings of Pudumaipittan), ed. Venkatachalapathy, A R (Nagercoil: Kalachchuvadu Pathippagam, 1998) 102.
16. Ibid.

CHRONOLOGY

1906:	Pudumaippittan is born at Thiruppathirippuliyur, Kadalur District, Tamilnadu to Sri V Chokkalingam Pillai, a tahsildar, and Smt Parvathammal, on April 25. His early education was at Senji, Tindivanam and Kallakkurichi.
1918:	He moved to Tirunelveli and studied at Hindu College. Got a belated BA degree in 1931.
1932:	Marriage to Kamala (1917-1995) of Thiruvananthapuram in July.
1933:	His first published piece, "Gulab Jan Kathal" in the nationalist periodical *Gandhi*, edited by T S Chokkalingam, in October.
1934:	Moved to Chennai in April. Began to publish extensively – short stories, essays and reviews – in the literary renaissance journal *Manikkodi*.
1934 August- **1935 February:**	He was the sub-editor at *Oozhiyan*, the nationalist weekly edited by Roya Chokkalingam.
1935 July- **1943 September:**	He was the sub editor at the daily *Dinamani*. Published a number of trenchant book reviews, engaged in polemics, translated a number of short stories from around the world. A steep drop in his short stories.

1939:	*Ulagathu Sirukathaigal,* his translation of short stories from around the world is published. His political biographies of Mussolini and Hitler published.
1940:	*Pudumaippittan Kathaikal,* his first collection of short stories published.
1941-1946	Many of his later stories published in *Kalaimagal.*
1943:	In September, resigned en masse with other sub editors of *Dinamani* in solidarity with T S Chokkalingam, the editor, due to infringement of editorial rights by the management.
1944:	Assistant editor at the daily *Dinasari* founded by T S Chokkalingam. Quits after a year.
1945-47:	Entered the film world and works for *Avvaiyar* and *Kamavalli.*
1946:	Only daughter Dinakari born in April.
1947-1948:	At Pune working on M K Tyagaraja Bhagavathar's *Rajamukti.* Is diagnosed with tuberculosis in April.
1948:	Returned to his wife's hometown, seriously ill, in May.
1948:	Died on June 30.'

BIBLIOGRAPHY

Pudumaippittan's works

1. *Pudumaippittan Katturaigal.*   1954
2. *Kanmani Kamalavukku.*   1994
3. *Pudumaippittan Padaippugal*   1988
   (Collected works of Pudumaippittan).
4. *Annai Itta Thi* (Uncollected and Unpublished   1998
   Writings of Pudumaippittan), ed. Venkatachalapathy, A R.
5. *Pudumaippittan Kathaikal* (The Complete Stories of   2000
   Pudumaippittan) A chronological variorum edition with
   critical notes and appendices, ed. Venkatachalapathy, A R.
6. *Pudumaippittan Katturaigal* (Second volume of the critical
   2002
   edition of Pudumaippittan's collected works.)
   ed. Venkatachalapathy, A R.

Critical works on Pudumaippittan

1. *Pudumaippittan* (A biography of Pudumaippittan.   1951
   Reprinted several times.) Ragunathan, T M C.
2. *Tamilil Sirukathai: Varalaarum   Valarcchiyum,*
   Sundararajan,   1977
   P G & Sivapathasundaram, S, Madras: Christian
   Literature Society.
3. *Manikkodi Kalam,* Ramaiah, B S.   1980
4. *Pudumaippittan Ilakkiyattadam,* Krishnaswamy, Pa (ed.).
   1995
5. "Tamizhukku naviina paarvai tandavar"   1998
   Sundara Ramaswamy in *Dinamani* (30 June 1998).

6. *Pudumaippittan Kathaikal: Vimarsanangalum Vishamathanangalum* 1999
   (A polemic about criticism of Pudumaippittan's works.)
   Ragunathan, T M C.
7. *Pudumaippittanin Kayittraravu.* Rajamarthandan,   2000
   A, Chennai: Tamilini.
8. *Pudumaippittan enum Brahmarakshas.* Raj Gouthaman.
   2000
   Chennai: Tamilini.

Pudumaippittan's Tamilnadu

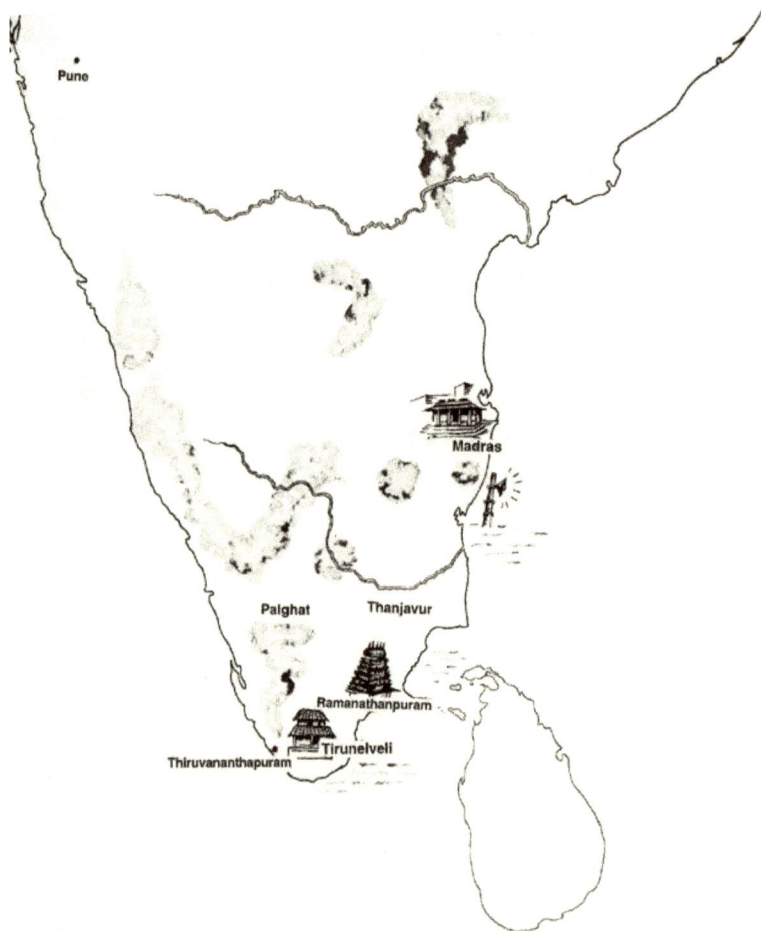

Lakshmi Holmström, freelance writer, critic and translator, is the author of Indian Fiction in English: the Novels of R K Narayan, editor of The Inner Courtyard: Short Stories by Indian women, and co-editor of Writing from India, a collection of Indian stories for young readers. Her re-telling of the fifth century Tamil narrative poems *Silappadikaram and Manimekalai* was published in 1996. She has translated works of many contemporary Tamil writers including Ashokamitran: *Water,* Mauni: *A Writers' Writer,* Ambai: *A Purple Sea*, Na Muthuswamy: Neermai. She has also translated *Karukku*, the autobiography of Baama, for which she received the Crossword Award for Translation 2000.

Marudu Trotsky, a former student of the College of Arts & Crafts, Chennai, is among the first practitioners of computer art and has used animation and digital art for creating special effects in a number of advertisement films and feature films. He has been instrumental in introducing a contemporary style for story illustrations in magazines, thereby opening new avenues for aspiring young artists.

K S Kulkarni (1916-1994) ranked among the pioneers of modern Indian art. A student of the J J School of Arts, he was a political activist during the Quit India movement. Immediately after independence, he revolted against the sentimental nationalism in the art of the Bengal School and its wide sphere of influence. He founded the Delhi Shilpi Chakra and the Triveni Kala Sangam and was a major influence upon the Delhi art scene.
Medieval Indian sculptures have greatly influenced his works. He was equally at ease while adapting to the mores of some of the Western Masters as while working within the Indian tradition. In his own words, " ... I am interested in the

universalizing of the human spirit .... My art springs from within and flows from my perception of the rhythm of life around me in the global context."

Gallerie Ganesha aspires to promote young and promising talents, generate an awareness for art by constant exposure to high quality works of Art, give exposure to skilled and dedicated Artists of yesteryears who went unnoticed due to lack of merlia attention and to provide a platform for interaction between the artist and the viewer.

After more than a decade of its existence, the Gallery can with some measure of pride, take credit for achieving the above objectives. Gallerie Ganesha today offers a large selection of paintings, sculptures, drawings, lithographs, serigraphs, prints, etchings, photographs, et cetera created by artists of fame and promise.

ABOUT KATHA

India has always been a land of storytellers. Over the centuries, we have honed the fine art of telling the short story – be it in our epics, our mythologies, our folktales or in our more recent writings. Told by traditional Katha vachaks, village storytellers and one's favourite grandmother, we have all heard stories that have taught us our values, our morals, our culture. "Katha" or the narrative is a special legacy that continues to exist in our country as a rich and fascinating tradition, moving with grace and felicity from the oral traditions to the written texts, from the heard word to the read.

We at Katha endeavour to spread the joy of reading, knowing, and living amongst adults and children, the common reader and the neo-literate. Katha has striven to establish a code of excellence in all that it does, to enhance the quality of life in every project it has attempted.

Katha's main objective is **to enhance the pleasures of reading for children and adults,** for experienced readers as well as for those who are just beginning to read. And, inter alia, to –

* Stimulate an interest in lifelong learning that will help the child grow into a confident, self-reliant, responsible and responsive adult.
* Help break down gender, cultural and social stereotypes.
* Encourage, foster excellence, and applaud quality literature and translations in and between the various Indian languages.

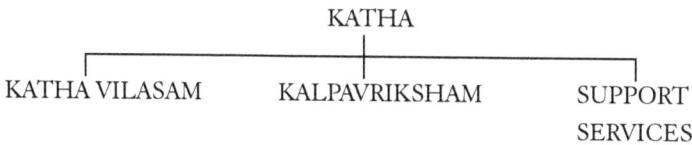

```
                         KATHA
          ┌───────────────┼───────────────┐
KATHA VILASAM      KALPAVRIKSHAM        SUPPORT
                                        SERVICES
```

KATHA VILASAM: The Story Research and Resource Centre was created in September 1989 with the following main purposes:
* To help capacity build in writers, translators and editors. To organize and promote, wherever required, the study of those subjects through lectures, demonstrations/workshops etc.

- To offer a decentralized research and a centralized documentation service on Indian literature, focusing on short fiction. The idea is to collect and have for larger use research papers, writings and other forms of scholarship on writers and writings.
- To publish quality translations of good writings from the various Indian languages, in English.

These goals have crystallized in the development of the following areas of activities:

- **Katha Books:** Publishing of Quality Translations
- **Academic Publishing Programme:** Books for teaching of translation and Indian fiction
- **Applauding Excellence:** The Katha Awards for fiction, translation, editing
- **Kathakaar:** The Centre for Children's Literature
- **Katha Barani:** The Translation Resource Centre
- **Katha Sethu:** Building bridges between India and the outside world
  - **The Katha Translation Exchange Programme**
  - **Translation Contests**
- **Kanchi:** Katha National Institute of Translation was started in 1994 with the Vak Initiative for enhancing the pool of translators between the various bhashas.
  - **Katha Academic Centres.** In various universities across the country
  - **The Faculty Enhancement programme.** Workshops, seminars, discussions
  - **Sishya:** Katha Clubs in colleges; workshops, certificate courses, events and contests
  - **The Katha Internship programme** for students from outside India
  - **Storytellers Unlimited:** Stotytelling – the Art and Craft
  - **KathaRasa:** Performances, Art Fusion, events. Katha Centre Activities

KALPAVRIKSHAM: The Centre for Sustainable Learning was created in

September 1989 with the following main purposes:

- To foster quality education for children from nonliterate families that is relevant and fun
- To develop teaching/learning materials that see the story as the basis, for fostering lifelong learning skills and knowledge in our children that will make classroom teaching rememberable and understandable.
- To find, foster, and applaud good teaching of our children, through inservice and preservice training.

These goals crystallized in the development of the following areas of activities:

- **Katha Khazana**
  - **Katha Student Support Centre.**
  - **Katha Public School**
  - **Katha School of Entrepreneurship**
  - **KITES.** Katha Information Technology and eCommerce School
  - **Iccha Ghar. The Intel Computer Clubhouse @ Katha**
  - **Hamara Gaon.** Community revitalization and economic resurgence.
  - **The Mandals:** Maa, Bapu, Balika, Balak, Danadini
  - **The Clubs:** Inducement to activity clubs like Gender Club, Mensa Club etc.
  - **KathaRasa,** Artistic education, performances, events.
- **Shakti Khazana:** Skills upgradation. Income generation activities. The Khazana Coop.
- **Kalpana Vilasam:** Regular research and development of teaching/ learning materials, curricula, syllabi, content
  - **Teacher training.**
  - **TaQeEd — The Teachers Alliance for Quality eEducation.**
- **Tamasha'S World!**
  - **Tamasha! the Children's magazine**
  - *Dhammakdhum!*
  - *www.tamasha.org*
  - **ANU — Animals, Nature and YOU!**

Paresh Maity   *105cm x 105cm, Oil on Canvas, 2002*

'NAYIKA'

GALLERIE GANESHA
E-557, Greater Kailash-II, New Delhi-110048
Phone: 6447306, 6446043
Email : shobha@del3.vsnl.net.in www.gallerieganesha.com

BE A FRIEND OF KATHA

If you feel strongly about Indian literature, you belong with us! KathaNet, an invaluable network of our friends, is the mainstay of all our translationorelated activities. We are happy to invite you to join this ever-widening circle of translation activists. Katha, with limited financial resources, is propped up by the unqualified enthusiasm and the indispensable support of nearly 5000 dedicated women and men.

We are constantly on the lookout for people who can spare the time to find stories for us, and to translate them. Katha has been able to access mainly the literature of the major Indian languages. Our efforts to locate resource people who could make the lesser-known literatures available to us have not yielded satisfactory results. We are specially eager to find Friends who could introduce us to Bhojpuri, Dogri, Kashmiri, Maithili, Manipuri, Nepali, Rajasthani and Sindhi fiction.

Do write to us with details about yourself, your language skills, the ways in which you can help us, and any material that you already have and feel might be publishable under a Katha programme. All this would be a labour of love, of course' But we do offer a discount of 20% on all our publications to Friends of Katha.

Write to us at -

Katha
A-3 Sarvodaya Enclave
Sri Aurobindo Marg   Call us at: 4441 6600, 4141 6624
New Delhi 110017   or E-mail us at: info@katha.org

www.ingramcontent.com/pod-product-compliance
Lightning Source LLC
Chambersburg PA
CBHW031948080426
42735CB00007B/308